HOW TO BE A WIFE AND IMPROVE YOUR MARRIAGE

Simple and amazing guides to having a blissful marriage and enjoying your husband in a lasting Marriage in Spring, Summer, Winter and Fall. Marriage is in seasons and the major purpose of this book is to help you and your spouse understand each season and conquer them with love.

Samantha Nunez Chapman

Samantha Nunez Chapman

HOW TO BE A BETTER WIFE AND IMPROVE YOUR MARRIAGE

Samantha Nunez Chapman

Copyright © 2022 by Samantha Nunez Chapman

All rights reserved. No part of this publication may be reproduced, distributed, or transmitted in any form or by any means, including photocopying, recording, or other electronic or mechanical methods, without the prior written permission of the publisher, except in the case of brief quotations embodied in critical reviews and certain other noncommercial uses permitted by copyright law.

Table of Contents

INTRODUCTION 6
CHAPTER ONE 10
   The Heart of Emotional Intelligence 10
CHAPTER TWO 25
   The Art of Empathetic Listening 25
CHAPTER THREE 37
   Take Responsibility 37
      My realization came when I understood that the heaps of laundry weren't a sentence to spend the rest of my days in a cluttered 39
      Create a vision board or a scene that represents your ideal situation (with or without your Husband) 40
      It's the same way with your relationship with your spouse. Choose a new location for your marriage if you want to be in a different place in your connection with your husband. 40
CHAPTER FOUR 47
   Color-code your calendar 47
CHAPTER FIVE 57
   Have The Determination to Maintain a Cheerful State of Mind When Married 57
   Self-awareness 57
   Communication 62
CHAPTER SIX 70
   Soften your startup 70
CHAPTER SEVEN 82
   Use the K.N.O.W. Method 82
CHAPTER EIGHT 95

Align your priorities with those of your Husband. 95

CHAPTER NINE 103
Create a way of talking that everyone can understand and that makes them feel like they are being heard 103

CHAPTER TEN 112
It All Starts With Cultivating A Positive Relationship With Oneself 112

CHAPTER ELEVEN 121
Make A Conscious Effort to Date And Get to Know One Another 121

CHAPTER TWELVE 131
Communicate Your Needs 131

CHAPTER THIRTEEN 139
Tell Him How Good He Is In Bed 139

CHAPTER FOURTEEN 146
Aid His Friendships 146

CHAPTER FIFTEEN 153
Let Go of Your Phone 153

CHAPTER SIXTEEN 162
Give Him Some Space 162

CHAPTER SEVENTEEN 169
Help Him Achieve His Goals 169

CHAPTER EIGHTEEN 176
Help Him Achieve His Goals 176

CHAPTER NINETEEN 183
Rise And Shine Before He Does 183

CHAPTER TWENTY 192
Encourage Him to Maintain a Healthy Lifestyle 192

CHAPTER TWENTY ONE 201
Before You Say Something Hurtful, Do A Gut Check 201

CHAPTER TEWNTY TWO 212
Take His Mother Out to Lunch 212

CHAPTER TWENTY-THREE 219
Be Your Man's Best Friend 219

CHAPTER TWENTY-FOUR 227
Making Time for Him 227

CHAPTER TWENTY-FIVE 235
Start Sex 235

LEND YOUR VODY OUR VOICE 242

ACKNOWLEDGEMENT 243

ABOUT THE AUTHOR 245

INTRODUCTION

WHILE NO MARRIAGE IS PERFECT, THERE IS ALWAYS ROOM FOR IMPROVEMENT.
Marriage requires effort on both sides, and both people must commit to improving and growing together.

That is why Samantha Nunez Chapman bestowed upon us the knowledge of how to be a better wife and improve your marriage effortlessly.
Create a vision or an ideal scene with or without your husband.
A vision board, also known as an ideal scene, can be a fun way to visualize where you want your marriage to go. Choose imagery that evokes the feelings you want to share or that depicts the experiences you wish to have together.

Imagine yourself and your spouse at a fork in the road with no clear path ahead. Imagine if there was a lighthouse pointing the way to a future in which each step you took deepened your relationship with your partner. The goal of this book, "How to be a Better Wife and Improve Your Marriage," is to serve as that roadmap. This story dives deeply into the complex dance of connection to transform as much as inform.

Matrimony is a beautiful and demanding journey that two souls undertake together. The everyday moments that unite two hearts hold the substance of this union rather than the glorious displays of affection. This book is designed for people who want to explore these times more deeply, grasp the nuanced aspects of being a spouse, and improve their marriage. This is intended for recently married couples starting this journey, enthusiastic learners looking to strengthen their relationship, seasoned partners hoping to reignite their marriage, and all relationship builders.
The straightforward yet essential issue that guides our investigation is this: How can each of us individually support a successful marriage? The solution is not in one action but in a sequence of deliberate, mindful behaviours that honour value and respect our relationships. We set out to create a solid foundation of love and respect

by travelling together through the pages of this book on a voyage of self-discovery, understanding, and emotional development.

Numerous people's stories of navigating the ups and downs of marriage, just like you, form the beating heart of this story. These tales act as a mirror and a map, reflecting our everyday experiences and offering direction for developing closer relationships, from the thrill of first love to the difficulties that put our relationships to the test. Carefully constructed, each chapter covers essential facets of married life, providing helpful guidance, real-life experiences, and thoughtful activities to foster better communication, increase emotional closeness, and fortify the union.

We explore the importance of accepting accountability for our deeds and the transformational potential of direct, honest communication. A lively, healthy relationship depends on the skill of starting sex, a topic that is sometimes cloaked in mystery and discomfort. This topic is sensitively and perceptively discussed. The book urges couples to set clear priorities, enjoy each other's company, and deal with life's obstacles gracefully and with resiliency.

The idea of "becoming a better wife" is redefined throughout these pages. Being a carer means something other than losing oneself or living up to an antiquated standard. It's really about developing a relationship based on love, respect, and mutual learning rather than competing against one another. This book challenges you to examine your behaviours, attitudes, and presumptions in light of how they affect your relationships. It is an invitation to look within.

This story is all about practicality. In addition to its philosophical observations on love and connection, this book provides concrete, doable strategies to improve your marriage. The time-management techniques offered range from learning a new language to strengthening relationships to color-coding calendars to manage time together. These aren't one-size-fits-all answers but rather a place to start a discussion about what makes your particular relationship function best between you and your spouse.

In the ensuing chapters, we address the intricacies of intimacy, the subtleties of communication, and the skill of compromise. We talk about how important it is to keep a positive outlook, how flexibility in thought and behaviour is beneficial, and how self-awareness is essential in our relationships. The knowledge that marriage is a dynamic, ever-changing journey and that every day offers a fresh chance for development and connection informs every discussion topic.

This book's tone is purposefully intimate and human since marriage is very private. Real-world experiences are the source of the stories and examples offered, which serve as both cautionary tales and sources of inspiration. The intention is never to instruct but to guide, never to order but to offer suggestions, always keeping in mind that the reader is the one who makes the final decision.

Furthermore, this book recognises various marriages and partnerships, realising that each is as distinct as the people who make up the union. The suggestions and information are designed to be flexible, enabling each couple's unique requirements and situation to be tailored accordingly. It's an ever-expanding tool that provides guidance and assistance during the different phases of your married life.

As a guide for those seeking a more satisfying marriage, "How to be a Better Wife and Improve Your Marriage" is more than just a book. It serves as evidence of the transformative potential of marriage, the strength of love, and the value of dedication. This book provides a new outlook on what it means to be a friend, lover, and partner, regardless of where you are in your path or how long you have been doing it.

Keep in mind that the route you take as you turn these pages.

A step towards compassion, understanding, and love is the first step towards a healthier marriage. You're encouraged to take that first step, to embrace the pleasures and difficulties of matrimony, and to experience the deep fulfilment that accompanies creating a life together with every chapter. Greetings, and welcome to your path of bettering your marriage and becoming a better wife. **Let's get started.**

Discover helpful insights in the following pages.

CHAPTER ONE

The Heart of Emotional Intelligence

Knowing What Emotional Intelligence Is

KNOWING EMOTIONAL INTELLIGENCE (EI) IS THE FOUNDATION OF A SUCCESSFUL marriage. Emotional intelligence (EI) is the capacity to identify, understand, control, and navigate one's own emotions and those of other people. When two people are married and their lives are deeply entwined, emotional intelligence (EI) becomes not simply a skill but also a crucial requirement. It is the lighthouse that helps couples navigate the ups and downs of their emotional tides so that their union sails smoothly.

Self-awareness is the starting point for the development of emotional intelligence. This is the capacity to comprehend your feelings, to see how they impact your ideas and behaviour, and to see how they impact others around you, particularly your partner. Imagine a situation where one partner had a difficult day and returned home. A spouse with emotional intelligence may be able to identify minor signs of concern, such as a shift in body language or a calmer manner. The first step in creating a supportive atmosphere where open communication and empathy are the rule rather than the exception is recognising these signs.

Another critical aspect of EI in a marriage is self-regulation. It's the capacity to control your feelings and know when to let them out. Think about the difference between reacting angrily to a misunderstanding immediately and pausing to collect yourself, assess the situation, and select a more favourable course of action. The latter, driven by self-control, keeps the issue from worsening and helps the relationship develop a patient and understanding culture.

Empathy is the foundation of emotional intelligence, especially when it comes to the dynamics of marriage. It is the capacity to truly comprehend one's partner's thoughts, feelings, and viewpoints by placing oneself in their position. Empathy allows partners to connect deeply by bridging the distance between their hearts. When one partner genuinely understands what the other is going through, true support and solidarity are expressed instead of just compassion.

In the context of emotional intelligence, social skills are the capacity to navigate and impact the emotional terrain of interpersonal encounters constructively. Establishing and upholding trust, resolving conflicts amicably, and communicating effectively are all aspects of social skills necessary for a happy marriage. Couples with these abilities can weather the highs and lows with grace and resiliency.

Developing Emotional Intelligence (EI) in your marriage can be achieved through regular mindfulness exercises. Focusing entirely on your companion during active listening can help you better understand their viewpoint. Expressing gratitude to one another regularly helps to fortify your emotional connection. Emotional check-ins can be scheduled to make both partners feel acknowledged and appreciated. Furthermore, you can strengthen your relationship with your partner by actively exercising empathy, genuinely interested in their experiences, and asking them how they feel.

Developing these aspects of emotional intelligence in your marriage is an ongoing process of learning and development rather than a one-time event. As newlyweds and those seeking to deepen their relationship follow this path, they will discover that the Emotional Intelligence base they establish will improve their marital contentment and offer a robust platform for overcoming obstacles in life as a couple. In fact, emotional intelligence is the foundation for enduring love and a successful connection, given its enormous influence on both individual and interpersonal well-being.

Cultivating a robust and resilient marriage requires an understanding of emotional intelligence. The fundamental ability allows us to be aware of, comprehend, and control our feelings while sympathetically identifying and responding to our partner's feelings. This seemingly straightforward capacity has significant effects on the dynamics of marital harmony.

Fundamentally, emotional intelligence (EQ) is the ability to have deep and meaningful conversations that go beyond the surface, creating a connection based on understanding, respect, and unwavering support. Consider how different you might react, for instance, to a partner's unsatisfactory workday. A high EQ strategy includes:
- Paying attention to what they are frustrated about.
- Providing consolation without leaping to solutions.
- Accepting their emotions without passing judgment.
- They feel recognised and supported by this answer, which validates their experience.

Additionally, EQ improves our ability to resolve conflicts amicably. Any relationship will inevitably have conflicts; however, how these arguments are handled will decide how they affect the partnership. Couples with a high degree of emotional intelligence can resolve problems by emphasising personal development and growth more than winning arguments. It helps us handle delicate subjects with caution and ensures that, even when we disagree, we respect one another's opinions and feelings.

Emotional intelligence also allows us to communicate our needs and desires constructively and straightforwardly. Finding the right balance between assertiveness and vulnerability is critical to fostering open communication that builds trust in a relationship. Expressing gratitude for each other's efforts in the relationship—from appreciating routine chores to recognising the emotional labour each spouse contributes—is a straightforward but effective illustration of this. This realisation dramatically raises marital satisfaction by fostering a culture of thankfulness in the union.

Gaining emotional intelligence is a journey that calls for reflection, practice, and a dedication to improvement. The first steps are being self-aware, knowing your emotional triggers, and realising how they impact your relationships with your partner. After that, it's about developing the capacity to hold off on acting and make decisions that are consistent with the kind of partner you want to be.

Setting aside time for daily check-ins, where each spouse discusses something they felt strongly about that day, without interruption or judgement from the other, is one practical exercise to improve emotional intelligence in marriages. Empathy swapping is an additional activity in which partners voice a worry or problem alternately. At the same time, the other makes a concerted effort to understand the circumstances from their point of view.

In summary, emotional intelligence is crucial for managing a marriage, not merely helpful. It supports every conversation, argument, and intimate moment spent with a spouse. Marital relationships can be improved by developing EQ, which converts obstacles into chances to strengthen bonds and love. Let's keep in mind that the core of emotional intelligence is recognising and controlling emotions and doing so in a way that strengthens and elevates our most valued connection as we navigate the many terrains of marriage.

Emotional intelligence's place in marriage

Emotional intelligence in marriage is more than just knowing how to identify your feelings; it's also about managing, comprehending, and reacting appropriately to your partner's feelings. When two people unite in marriage to share their lives, emotional intelligence becomes essential to a meaningful and satisfying partnership.

Navigating the intricate emotional terrain of marriage requires high emotional intelligence or EQ. It involves more than just being conscious of your emotions; it also involves sensing and appreciating your partner's feelings. This comprehension creates a supportive atmosphere where both parties feel heard, seen, and appreciated.

Imagine the following: a standard argument that might break out between partners. One could feel inclined to react dismissively or defensively, putting their viewpoint ahead of their partner's. However, a spouse with vital emotional intelligence would handle the matter differently. They would attentively listen, attempting to comprehend their partner's point of view without passing judgment or taking offence right away. This is acknowledging the emotions of both parties and addressing them rather than repressing one's feelings.

Emotional intelligence depends on effective communication in a marriage. It's about being honest about your thoughts and feelings while considering how others may interpret you. This entails speaking in a respectful and considerate manner, even when there is disagreement. Sayings like "Your feelings are valid" or "I understand where you're coming from" can defuse a potentially explosive situation and start a productive conversation.

Recognising emotional bids, or our often subtle attempts to establish a connection with our partner, is another aspect of emotional intelligence. A simple glance, a kind touch, or a question about someone's day could qualify as a bid. Demonstrating to your partner that they are significant to you can deepen the emotional connection by carefully considering and accepting their proposals.

Moreover, empathy—the capacity to put oneself in another person's shoes—is a component of emotional intelligence in marriage. Let's say your significant other has had a difficult day. Empathy prompts you to offer assistance by listening, empathising with their suffering, or offering consolation instead of concentrating on your personal needs or frustrations at that particular time.

Emotional intelligence in conflict management is another essential component. Any partnership will inevitably have conflicts, but how they are resolved will decide how booming the union is. High emotional intelligence is demonstrated by approaching arguments with the intention of understanding rather than winning and looking for solutions that benefit both parties.

Ultimately, developing emotional intelligence in a married relationship is a continuous endeavour. It calls for perseverance, repetition, and a sincere desire to improve. It's about recognising each other's accomplishments, growing from our errors, and never giving up on comprehending and satisfying each other's emotional needs.

It is impossible to overestimate emotional intelligence's significant influence on a marriage. It is the cornerstone of a solid, long-lasting relationship in which both parties experience a profound sense of worth, understanding, and connection. By developing our emotional intelligence, we strengthen our union and serve as role models for those around us, leaving a legacy of happy, healthy marriages.

Building a solid, long-lasting marriage requires understanding the emotional intelligence (EI) component. The capacity to identify, comprehend, and regulate our own emotions and those of others is known as emotional intelligence, and it is essential to our ability to connect, communicate, and work through problems with our partners. This realisation is significant for recently married couples, eager students, seasoned spouses, and anyone dedicated to enhancing their relationships.

The ability of both parties to empathically tune into each other's emotional needs, concerns, and desires is at the core of any successful marriage. When we possess emotional intelligence, we may interpret our partner's statements based on their intents and feelings in addition to what they are saying. This makes it possible for us to react to the emotional undercurrents of discourse in addition to its obvious content.

Active listening is a real-world application of emotional intelligence. It entails giving the speaker your attention instead of just hearing what is being said. It's about using every sense to listen. When one spouse expresses worries about their employment, for example, emotional intelligence helps the other listen empathetically, recognise the emotions involved, and provide support instead of leaping to conclusions or brushing the concerns off. Each individual feels appreciated and understood when using this method, which promotes a stronger bond and a sense of cooperation.

Furthermore, the constructive management of disputes depends heavily on emotional intelligence. Disagreements are a given in any marriage. Couples' relationship might be strengthened or weakened depending on how they resolve these arguments. High emotional intelligence partners know when to react calmly and identify their triggers. This helps them negotiate difficulties together. Even in the heat of the moment, they make an effort to comprehend their partner's point of view, which enables resolutions that consider both parties' wants and feelings.

Consider a situation where one partner feels ignored because of the other's demanding work schedule. With no intention of placing blame or condemnation, a partner with a high emotional intelligence (EI) could say, "I feel lonely when we don't spend much time together," as opposed to, "You never spend time with me." Instead of starting a fight, this statement facilitates a productive discussion about problems and solutions.

Acknowledging and expressing your thankfulness for your partner's and your relationship's positive qualities is another way to develop emotional intelligence. While taking ordinary acts of generosity and affection for granted is simple, recognising them deepens the emotional connection between spouses. A small gesture like saying "thank you" for making coffee in the morning or writing a note of appreciation for being an excellent listener can significantly impact a marriage's general level of happiness and satisfaction.

Developing emotional intelligence in a marriage requires ongoing learning and development rather than a one-time effort. It entails candid communication, consistent introspection, and a readiness to show vulnerability to one another. By placing a high priority on emotional intelligence, couples can establish a foundation of love, respect, and understanding that withstands life's ups and downs.

Developing solid and long-lasting relationships in marriage thus requires emotional intelligence, making it more than a benefit. It gives couples the skills to understand one another better, handle the challenges of a shared existence with grace, and develop a relationship that will not only last but also be rewarding for both.

Self-evaluation: Measuring emotional intelligence

Self-evaluation: For anyone devoted to marriage enhancement and personal development, determining your emotional intelligence quotient is essential. The foundation for comprehending and negotiating the intricate nuances of a relationship, especially the holy connection of marriage, is emotional intelligence (EQ). It's about identifying our feelings and those of our partner, controlling them sensibly, and handling conflict with compassion and understanding.

When starting this self-evaluation process, it's critical to remember that emotional intelligence is a collection of abilities that can be cultivated over time rather than an inborn quality. The objective is to pinpoint areas for development and progress rather than to pass judgment on oneself harshly. This investigation is an offering to your marriage, a dedication to cultivating a more profound, perceptive bond with your partner.

Understanding Your Emotional Habits

Start by noting how you feel in different circumstances. How do you respond when you're under pressure, happy, or stressed? Do specific trends show up? Understanding your emotional environment starts with identifying these patterns. It's similar to charting your emotional geography, figuring out what sets off powerful emotions, and comprehending how these feelings affect your decisions and thinking.

Recognising How You Affect Your Relationship

Your partner is greatly affected by the way you communicate your emotions. Think back to times when your partner was impacted by your feelings, both good and bad. Think about how your attitude affects everyone else in the house. Understanding the strength of your feelings will help you start controlling them so that they strengthen rather than damage your connection.

Putting Oneself in Your Partner's Shoes: Empathy

"Empathy serves as the cornerstone of emotional intelligence within a marriage." It entails fully sharing your feelings with your spouse, not just comprehending them. Consider things from your partner's point of view. Beneath those words, what hopes and what fears? Empathy creates a bridge between people's hearts, facilitating more accessible assistance and consolation during difficult situations.

Controlling Feelings During Disputes

Any relationship will inevitably experience conflict; however, how you handle your feelings during these moments determines the strength of your union. Gaining self-calming techniques, like walking, deep breathing, or mindfulness training, can help you handle conflict more rationally. A potential disagreement can be turned into a learning opportunity if you can learn to express your emotions positively without placing blame or offering criticism.

Gaining Emotional Resilience

Emotional agility is the capacity to adapt and purposefully deal with life's changes and obstacles. It entails having the capacity to change one's emotional state in reaction to the current circumstance. Developing this ability entails recognising unpleasant feelings, learning from them, and bouncing back from them instead of being mired in them.

Realistic Measures for Development

Maintain a Journal: Start recording your emotional reactions and the circumstances that lead to them. Over time, patterns will start to emerge, providing insights into your emotional responses and routines.

Request Input: Discuss how your feelings impact one another with your partner. This conversation might offer insightful viewpoints on areas in need of development. Put mindfulness into practice: Including mindfulness exercises in your routine can help you become more aware of the present moment and interact more deeply with your partner's feelings.

Acquire the Pause: Pause in a heated moment before responding. This small gesture can free you to respond with more consideration and compassion.
Honour Emotional Victories: Celebrate the times when you could control your emotions or demonstrate a great deal of empathy for your partner. Even the smallest of these successes contributes to a more emotionally savvy marriage.

As recently weds, interested students, seasoned partners, and relationship builders, remember that developing emotional intelligence in your marriage is an ongoing effort. It involves putting in little but steady effort to get to know and understand your partner better. By starting on this path of self-evaluation and emotional development, you're not just trying to be a better wife or husband; you're also trying to create a stronger, more durable marriage that will endure the test of time.

Chapter Summary

"The Heart of Emotional Intelligence," explores the vital part that emotional intelligence (EI) plays in enhancing and maintaining a happy marriage. First, emotional intelligence (EI) is defined as the capacity to identify, comprehend, control, and constructively use one's own emotions and those of others. To successfully navigate the challenges of married life, the chapter emphasises self-awareness, self-regulation, empathy, and social skills as the fundamental pillars of emotional intelligence (EI). It emphasises that improving one's emotional intelligence (EI) is a continuous process that greatly impacts resilience and marital contentment. Through exercises, realistic examples, and helpful advice, this chapter offers couples a road map for strengthening their emotional bond, communicating better, and creating a more solid and long-lasting marriage.

Important Points

Emotional Intelligence as a Marital Foundation: The chapter highlights the importance of emotional intelligence (EI) in building a caring and sympathetic connection and argues that it is essential for comprehending and negotiating the emotional dynamics inside a marriage.

Self-awareness and self-regulation: It describes how these qualities are essential for patiently and empathetically reacting to marital difficulties. Self-awareness is the knowledge of one's feelings; self-regulation is the capacity to control and express those feelings healthily.

Empathy: It is said that a key component of emotional intelligence and a means of strengthening the emotional tie between spouses is the capacity to comprehend and experience one's partner's feelings.

Social Skills in Marriage: This point addresses the role that social skills, including good communication and dispute resolution, play in preserving a strong and resilient marriage.

Practices for Developing Emotional Intelligence (EI): This chapter ends with some doable tactics for improving EI in marriage, such as emotional check-ins, expressing gratitude, active listening, and cultivating empathy via common experiences and understanding.

Important Takeaways

Developing emotional intelligence (EI) in marriage changes how couples interact, communicate, and support one another, resulting in a more fulfilling and long-lasting union.

The Function of Emotional Intelligence in Resolving Conflicts: Couples with high EI are better able to view conflicts as learning experiences rather than win-lose situations, which encourages positive solutions that consider both parties' wants and feelings.

It's All About Communication: Emotionally intelligent communication is essential for expressing needs, wants, and thanks, which improves appreciation and understanding between parties.

Key Emotional Needs: A successful partnership depends on partners identifying and meeting each other's emotional needs, which is made possible by emotional intelligence (EI).

It's Critical to Continue Developing Your EI: Developing emotional intelligence is an ongoing process in a marriage that requires constant work, introspection, and a desire to advance as a couple.

Practical Exercises

Establish daily emotional check-ins to encourage open communication and empathy. Give partners time each day to discuss their thoughts and experiences without interruption.

Exchange empathy by discussing issues or difficulties while the other partner concentrates on comprehending and feeling the speaker's point of view. This will improve understanding between the two people.

Journaling Emotional Reactions: Keep a record of your feelings in response to different circumstances, and then talk with your partner about it to find trends and places where your emotional awareness needs to improve.

Mindfulness exercises can help you become more aware of the present moment and strengthen your emotional bond with your partner.

Appreciation Ritual: Consistently show appreciation for each other's contributions to the partnership, fostering gratifying exchanges and strong emotional ties.

Time For Reflections

How do my emotional responses affect our relationship, and how can I control them better?

_____
_____
_____
_____
_____
_____
_____
_____
_____
_____
_____
_____

How can I more effectively comprehend and relate to my partner's emotional experiences?

What techniques can we use to enhance our communication, particularly amid disagreements?

How can we develop routines that support empathy and understanding on an emotional level?

How can I constantly improve my emotional intelligence to strengthen our marriage?

CHAPTER TWO

The Art of Empathetic Listening

Techniques for active listening

UNDERSTANDING YOUR PARTNER'S EMOTION AND INTENTION BEHIND their words, rather than just hearing them, is fundamental to empathic communication in marriages. This ability is crucial for anyone looking to strengthen their connection, newlyweds starting their life adventure together, and seasoned spouses adjusting to the ups and downs of marriage.

Giving your partner your whole attention is the first step towards understanding them. Distractions are common in today's hectic world but shouldn't happen during talks with your partner. Picture this: your significant other is telling you about their day, their difficulties, and their little triumphs. In this context, shutting off the TV, putting down your phone, and removing any other distractions that might make it difficult for you to participate in your partner's experiences entirely is what is meant by active listening. It all comes down to making your spouse feel heard and noticed, a haven amidst the daily grind.

Additionally, verbal and nonverbal cues are part of active listening. More than acknowledgements, nods, grins, and "uh-huhs" convey your interest in your partner and urge them to keep talking. These indicators show that you are participating emotionally in the conversation and physically present. Similarly, summarising your partner's words with something like, "It sounds like you had a really challenging day at work," shows that you are trying to comprehend the breadth of their experience. This method works wonderfully for giving your partner a sense of worth and understanding.

Furthermore, a key component of active listening is the skill of questioning. Unlike yes/no questions, open-ended questions allow your spouse to discuss their feelings and views in more detail. Inquiries such as "What was going through your mind when that happened?" and "How did that make you feel?" promote a deeper investigation of feelings and viewpoints. It involves removing the layers to uncover the essence of your partner's feelings and experiences.

Refusing to pass judgment or offer counsel immediately is another essential component of active listening. People frequently react automatically when faced with a shared issue by providing solutions or criticism. But to listen, you must be patient and aware that your partner could occasionally look for sympathy rather than solutions. This method creates a space where people feel comfortable being vulnerable and expressing their feelings without worrying about being judged or written off.

Finally, empathy is the foundation of active listening. It involves attempting to comprehend your spouse by seeing the world from their point of view, experiencing their emotions, and responding to them with that understanding. Empathy creates a shared emotional space that enhances the link between spouses by bridging the gap between separate experiences.

The practical use of these strategies can significantly impact the effectiveness of marital communication. Take the example of Anna and Marco, a recentlywed couple constantly fighting over what seemed to be insignificant issues. They found that by using active listening techniques, these arguments frequently resulted from deeper problems with feeling ignored and unappreciated. They were able to negotiate these seas with more empathy and understanding because active listening helped them turn their disagreements into chances for development and connection.

Becoming proficient at active listening requires practice. it is not a talent that can be acquired quickly. It takes patience, effort, and intentionality. However, its benefits in terms of forging a solid, sympathetic, and understanding bond are incalculable. By learning effective active listening practices, newlyweds, eager learners, and seasoned spouses alike can achieve a happy and long-lasting marriage.

Empathy Vs. Sympathy In Marital Communication

Even though they are frequently used synonymously in everyday speech, empathy and compassion have different connotations, particularly when discussing the complex subject of marital communication. This distinction becomes especially important for recently married couples, long-term partners, and couples who want to strengthen their bond. Knowing this contradiction is not only theoretical; it's a valuable tool that can change the dynamics of your relationship.

In a married relationship, empathy is putting yourself in your spouse's position, viewing the world from their perspective, and experiencing their emotions without passing judgment. Ultimately, it would help to put aside your opinions and feelings to connect with your partner's experience. This is an active process. When your significant other returns home discouraged due to a failure at work, empathy goes beyond simply acknowledging their dismay. It involves comprehending the feelings that underlie their experience—frustration, insecurity, or possibly fear of being inadequate—and relaying that knowledge back to them.

Even if it's a kind of emotional acceptance, sympathy keeps a certain distance. It's not with someone; it's feeling for them. If empathy is putting yourself in another person's shoes, sympathy recognises their misery from a distance. Using the previous example again, you could show sympathy or regret for your partner's work-related setback, but you wouldn't go so far as fully entering their emotional world.

These differences have significant practical ramifications for marital communication. Listening with empathy promotes a closer, more meaningful relationship. It lets your partner know you acknowledge, value, and—most importantly—feel their sentiments. This kind of communication strengthens trust, the cornerstone of any successful marriage. A level of vulnerability and closeness that cannot be attained by compassion alone is unlocked when partners have faith that they may express their deepest pleasures, worries, and hopes with one another without fear of judgment.

On the other hand, depending just on sympathy may unintentionally result in emotional walls. Despite their good intentions, empathetic reactions may be condescending or contemptuous. They could exacerbate the emotional distance between partners by making the sharer feel alone or misunderstood. This is not to argue that professions of sympathy have no place in a marriage; there are times when they can be consoling. But the secret is knowing when to express pity and when to go further with empathy.

Developing empathy takes time, practice, and, most importantly, active listening. It's not only listening to what your spouse says; it's also observing nonverbal clues, such as body language, tone of voice, and facial expressions, that reveal the entire range of their emotional condition. This degree of involvement strengthens the relationship that forms the foundation of your marriage by showing your partner that they have all of your attention and concern.

Empathetic listening is a skill that may be used regularly in even the simplest of situations. Think about the difference between saying, "I'm sorry you feel that way" (sympathy) and saying, "It sounds like you're feeling overwhelmed and unappreciated" in response to a complaint about domestic tasks. "Let us discuss how to divide these responsibilities more equitably" (empathy). The latter provides a road to resolution, reciprocal support, and acknowledgement of the emotions involved.

Numerous real-life instances exist where partners have used the power of sympathetic communication to turn a relationship around from the verge of divorce. These narratives frequently have one thing in common: a pivotal moment when one or both couples choose to actively listen and react empathetically, igniting a fresh awareness and respect for one another's feelings and experiences.

As we practise empathic listening, keep in mind that empathy is about comprehending issues rather than finding solutions. It's about establishing a secure environment in which feelings are welcomed and openly shared. Empathy adds strength to the bonds that tie spouses in the grand scheme of marriage, allowing them to celebrate sunshine and withstand storms with a level of connectedness that is beyond what pity can offer.

Activities to hone your listening abilities

Listening exercises are essential for strengthening the emotional connection between spouses and laying the groundwork for understanding and empathy in a marriage. To be a good listener, it's essential to do more than hear what your partner is saying; it also involves understanding all the feelings, intentions, and thoughts that go into those words. It takes commitment to truly comprehend your partner's point of view without passing judgment or feeling compelled to answer immediately. Here, we look at doable activities that will help you and your partner develop a profound degree of empathic listening.

Exercise 1: Introspection in Silence

First, schedule a moment when you and your companion are accessible from interruptions. One partner speaks about a sensation, idea, or experience for a few minutes. With no intention of interjecting, providing answers, or expressing opinions, the other partner listens carefully and focuses on taking in the information. Following the speaker's conclusion, the audience considers what they heard again, paying particular attention to the feelings and underlying ideas. This exercise aims to demonstrate that you genuinely understand your partner's point of view, not to agree or disagree.

Exercise 2: The Sensor of Emotions

The emphasis of this exercise is now on figuring out the feelings the words convey. Sometimes, when you're having a regular discussion, stop and ask each other, "What emotion do you think I'm feeling right now?" This encourages both parties to be more forthcoming with their emotional expressions and to listen more intently to their partner's underlying sentiments. It's a potent method for honing the skill of empathic listening—that is, acknowledging and validating one another's emotions.

Exercise 3: The Perspective Exchange

The Perspective Swap exercise aims to improve empathy by getting partners to consider circumstances from one another's point of view. After you've shared a story or a problem, ask your spouse to narrate the tale from your point of view, including the feelings and ideas they think you went through. After that, change roles. In addition to strengthening listening abilities, this exercise promotes a deeper emotional bond between partners by encouraging sincere attempts to comprehend one another's thoughts and emotions.

Exercise 4: The Challenge of Active Engagement

Active engagement aims to convey to your spouse that you are attentive and really interested in what they have to say. Try not to be distracted at all when you are having a conversation. This includes putting phones aside, shutting off the television, and maintaining eye contact. Demonstrate engagement by using non-verbal clues like nodding, facial expressions, and vocal affirmations like "I understand" or "Tell me more". With continued practice, this activity can significantly enhance the quality of your communication, giving each partner a sense of worth and inclusion.

Exercise 5: The Cultivator of Curiosity

Make it a habit to probe your partner with open-ended questions to elicit additional information about their feelings and thoughts. Try framing your queries to get detailed answers rather than posing a yes/no question. Say, "How did that make you feel?" as an example. and "What was going through your mind when that happened?" This exercise enhances your listening ability and comprehension of your partner's inner world.

These activities must be incorporated into your daily routine with patience, effort, and a shared commitment to personal development. Whether you're a newlywed pair, an eager learner, an experienced spouse, or someone looking to better your relationship, developing empathetic listening skills is ongoing. It has the potential to change your union significantly. It's about creating an understanding bridge that enhances your shared life experience while fortifying your relationship. Building a deeper, more meaningful relationship with your partner is possible by practising empathy every day. Empathetic listening is more than just a skill.

Chapter Summary

The practice of empathic listening in the context of marriage highlights its critical role in developing meaningful, long-lasting relationships between spouses. It thoroughly examines active listening strategies, the important distinction between sympathy and empathy in marriage communication, and useful activities to improve listening comprehension. The chapter describes how couples can improve their relationship by creating an atmosphere of empathy, understanding, and respect for one another through practical examples and suggestions. It is said that listening with empathy is a useful communication skill and a vital component of a happy, fulfilling relationship.

Important Points

In order to properly comprehend a partner's feelings and intentions, the chapter presents active listening as a multimodal strategy that includes giving your whole attention, observing verbal and nonverbal signs, asking open-ended questions, and refraining from passing judgement.

Sympathy vs. Empathy: It makes a clear contrast between sympathy, which keeps emotional distance, and empathy, which actively shares and understands a partner's sentiments. The chapter focuses on how empathy may strengthen marriages by transforming relationships.

Practical Activities: This set of five exercises helps couples get more adept at listening with empathy and encourages them to go deeply into each other's emotional lives.

Empathetic Listening as a Foundation: The chapter urges couples to practise and prioritise empathetic listening in their daily interactions, positioning it as a necessary skill for a successful, long-lasting marriage.

Important Takeaways

Comprehending Beyond Words: Effective communication and emotional closeness depend on understanding a partner's emotional state, not simply the words they use. Empathetic listening entails this.

The Value of Presence: Providing a partner with your whole attention creates a safe space for vulnerability and sincere connection. It also shows value and respect.

Open-ended questions: These are useful for eliciting more in-depth feelings and viewpoints as well as cultivating a culture of mutual understanding and inquiry in the relationship.

Non-Judgmental Stance: It's important to foster trust and openness by giving partners the impression that you genuinely listen to and support them, even when you don't offer quick fixes or criticism.

Empathy as a Relationship Strengthener: Empathetic listening helps couples overcome distance and strengthen their marriages in the face of difficulties by creating a shared emotional experience.

Practical Exercises

Introspection in Silence: Partners alternately share their ideas or emotions without interruption while one listens intently to the other, promoting a profound insight that doesn't require confirmation or refutation.

The Sensor of feelings: Regularly pause talks to recognise and communicate underlying feelings to improve emotional transparency and empathy.

The Perspective Exchange: By exchanging tales from one another's points of view, you can enhance empathy and connection by better understanding each other's emotional experiences.

The Difficulty of Active Engagement: Agree to have uninterrupted talks, demonstrating attentiveness through nonverbal indicators that validate each other's value.

The Curiosity Cultivator: Include open-ended inquiries in everyday conversations to probe each other's inner lives and foster greater empathy and understanding.

Reflection Time

When was the last time you experienced genuine listening from your spouse, and what particular behaviours resulted in that feeling?

_____
_____
_____
_____
_____
_____
_____
_____
_____
_____
_____
_____
_____

What distinguishes sympathising with your lover from empathising with them? Do you have an example of a circumstance when one strategy worked better?

_____
_____
_____
_____
_____
_____
_____
_____
_____
_____

Think back to a recent argument: Could the result have been different, and if so, in what way?

_____
_____
_____
_____
_____
_____
_____
_____
_____
_____

Which hands-on tasks do you find most difficult, and what does it tell you about how you listen now?

How do you make empathic listening a regular part of your life such that it becomes an inherent aspect of your relationship dynamic?

CHAPTER THREE

Take Responsibility

ACCEPTING ACCOUNTABILITY APPEARS AS A FUNDAMENTAL PRINCIPLE within matrimony, essential to the establishment and well-being of any enduring alliance. As we set out on this adventure, it is crucial to understand that marital duty goes beyond the simple allocation of domestic duties or financial obligations. It's a complex dance involving respect for one another, emotional support, and ongoing relationship maintenance.

Acknowledging one's part in the peace and discord within the marriage connection is necessary to accept responsibility. It encourages reflecting on how one's deeds, words, and even silences affect the dynamics of relationships. This could show up for recently married couples as figuring out how to acclimatise to living together for the first time or coordinating their life objectives. Conversely, seasoned partners may explore more profound levels of comprehension, recognising how years of shared experience have influenced their communication.

Imagine the following situation: communication disruptions. It's easy to assign blame, holding your partner responsible for miscommunications or unfulfilled expectations. Accepting responsibility, though, compels us to consider our part in these circumstances. Did we express our needs enough? Have we tried to understand our partner's viewpoint by listening intently? This introspection makes Growth possible, enabling partners to get past surface-level arguments and establish a more meaningful relationship.

Furthermore, accepting responsibility entails realising how one's emotional condition affects the connection—letting our emotions control how we behave when stressed or frustrated is easy. However, we can drastically change the nature of our relationship by consciously controlling our emotions and selecting to interact with our partner in a kind and understanding way. It turns possible confrontations into chances for understanding and bonding.

In real life, accepting responsibility can be developed through regular choices and behaviours. It's the choice to extend a warm greeting to your spouse at the end of a demanding day, the attempt to show appreciation for the little things in life, and the guts to own up to your mistakes and apologise. Even though they may not seem like much, these acts support the mutual respect and affection necessary for any successful marriage.

It may comfort eager learners and connection builders to know that accepting responsibility is a talent that can be honed with practice. Little steps, a dedication to introspection, and a willingness to change are the first steps. The marriage transforms from a collaboration into a haven of love and support where both parties feel respected and understood.

Women Actually Do Not See Things As They Are; We See Things As We Are

Choosing to see your husband as your greatest spiritual teacher allows you to see how each disagreement in your relationship becomes an opportunity for personal growth and to grow closer together in your marriage. Choosing to see your husband as your greatest spiritual teacher opens the door to seeing how each disagreement in your relationship becomes an opportunity for personal growth and for you to grow closer together in your marriage.

When I first got married, my husband and I used to have a lot of disagreements over how to keep our home clean and maintained properly. Despite the fact that I was a professional organizer, his idea of being orderly consisted in his heaps of clean and dirty clothes not overlapping on the floor of his bedroom. This drove me insane, and I felt completely overwhelmed by the mess he was making.

It was simple to lay the blame for my current state of mind on his shoulders at the time. The fact is that it didn't make me feel good, and it didn't assist with the clutter problem either. However, if you are willing to assume complete responsibility for your own feelings in a given situation, it is possible to achieve success. When two people are in a relationship, there is usually a significant amount of growth and healing that can occur.

The more I thought about the things that were going on in my own life that were being reflected back to me through this challenge, the more I realized how many projects and things were sitting in metaphorical piles waiting to be finished, much like the piles of clothes and papers that were strewn about our home.

My realization came when I understood that the heaps of laundry weren't a sentence to spend the rest of my days in a cluttered house, but rather an opportunity to slow down and consider the role that distraction was playing in my own life.

As soon as I realized what was going on, I became intrigued. After that, I committed to conquering my own distractions and mental clutter to address the issue. Finally, I took responsibility for my own "cleaning up" by having an open and honest talk with my husband in which I acknowledged my role in the upheaval and communicated vulnerably, honestly, and openly about how I was feeling and what sort of help I needed.

Following that, two things occurred relatively rapidly. First and foremost, the tiny messes about the house no longer seemed so serious to me. And second, without any prodding from me, my husband began to make a greater effort on a more frequent basis, and our home began to look and feel better as a consequence.

If you are willing to accept complete responsibility for your feelings and upset in your relationship, you will not only be a better wife, but closeness and trust will begin to grow, resulting in the flourishing of your relationship.

Create a vision board or a scene that represents your ideal situation (with or without your Husband)

As soon as you get in your car to go somewhere and you aren't sure how to get there, the first thing you do is enter the address of the destination into the GPS on your phone or the navigation system in your car. Being unable to locate the location due to a lack of knowledge of its address will make getting there quite difficult.

It's the same way with your relationship with your spouse. Choose a new location for your marriage if you want to be in a different place in your connection with your husband.

A vision board or an ideal scene can be a fun approach to paint a picture of where you want your marriage to go in terms of goals and expectations. When choosing pictures for your wedding, consider images that symbolize experiences you want to share or that express the sensations you want to experience together.
Add words that symbolize the characteristics you want your marriage to have or the principles you want to abide by as a husband and wife as well. Place your vision board in a prominent location where you will view it daily. When you glance at a vision board, you are essentially engaging in visualization throughout the day, which is why they are effective.

Things are created from ideas. Within a short period, you'll begin to wonder if your name is Alice and that you've just "passed through the vision board," as you'll find yourself in your very own personal wedded wonderland.
P.S. Your husband doesn't need to participate for this to be successful. Take advantage of this opportunity by gathering a bottle of wine and your favorite Spotify music, then be ready for an unforgettable evening together!

Chapter Summary

The transforming potential of accountability in the atmosphere of matrimony. It emphasises that taking responsibility involves more than just allocating tasks or making financial contributions; it also involves showing respect, providing emotional support, and making the ongoing effort necessary to maintain the relationship. It shows how recognising one's part in the relationship's harmony and discord may result in growth, greater understanding, and a more meaningful connection through real-world circumstances and personal tales. The chapter also presents the idea of seeing marital difficulties as chances for growth on a personal level and greater unity with one's spouse.

Important Points

The Basis of Accountability: Taking ownership of one's actions, including providing emotional support, respect, and relationship upkeep, is essential to a marriage's health and durability.

Effects of Words and Deeds: Acknowledging how one's actions, words, and even nonverbal clues impact a relationship's dynamics promotes individual and group development.

Emotional regulation is approaching relationships with kindness and understanding and realising how one's emotional state affects the partnership.

Practical Use: Expressing gratitude, accepting responsibility for errors, and actively fostering a healthy environment in the partnership are all practical steps towards accepting responsibility.

Future Vision: A vision board for the marriage can help create a common direction and stronger bond by encouraging both spouses to align their objectives and aspirations.

Important Takeaways

Personal Development via Partnership: Seeing your partner as a spiritual mentor might help you turn arguments into chances for growth and fortify your bond.

The Significance of Introspection: realising how you respond and feel in particular circumstances reflects your struggles and opportunities for development.

Conversation as a Resolution Tool: Addressing problems and promoting understanding between parties requires open, sincere, and vulnerable conversation.

Self-sufficiency in Collective Visioning: There is an unnecessary and optional need to participate in creating a vision for the marriage, demonstrating the value of individual initiative in improving relationships.

The Subtlety of Influence: Small, regular acts and attitude adjustments can greatly impact the general quality and direction of a marriage.

Practical Exercises

Journaling for Reflection: Every week, consider how your words and deeds have affected your marriage and identify areas that need work.

Emotional Awareness Practice: Make it a daily habit to assess your emotional condition before speaking with your spouse. Try to remain composed and empathic throughout these exchanges.

Appreciation Diary: To promote positivism, journal the qualities you value in your spouse and share entries with them after each week.

Making a Vision Board: Whether you do this alone or with a partner, make a vision board that reflects your aspirations and goals for your union. You can use it as a daily reminder of your road together.

Exercise in Active Listening: Engage in active listening throughout conversations, concentrating on fully comprehending your partner's viewpoint without pre-arranging your reply while they speak.

Reflection Time

What aspects of my behaviour and communication style influence my marriage's harmony or discord?

_____
_____
_____
_____
_____
_____
_____
_____
_____
_____
_____

How have I let my emotions get in my interactions with my spouse, and what can I do better?

_____
_____
_____

Samantha Nunez Chapman

Can you think of an instance where I accepted complete responsibility for my part in a disagreement? If so, what happened?

Can you think of an instance where I accepted complete responsibility for my part in a disagreement? If so, what happened?

How does the idea that my partner is a spiritual mentor affect how I see arguments and difficulties in our marriage?

What does my dream marriage entail, and how can I begin pursuing this goal right now?

Samantha Nunez Chapman

CHAPTER FOUR

Color-code your calendar

An expert in modern management once said,
"Tell me what you value and I might believe you, but show me your calendar and your bank statement and I'll show you what you value."

DEPENDING ON ONE'S VIEWPOINT AND THE STATE OF THEIR MARRIAGE, deciding to go on a month-long trip to have sex every day may seem like an exciting opportunity or an intimidating task. Nevertheless, it's an investigation that can, in a manner that few other experiences can match, strengthen bonds, promote closeness, and reveal the details of a relationship. That's a brave step but full of chances for development, comprehension, and unrestrained happiness.

Consider a couple who have become mired in the routine of everyday existence. The light that appeared unquenchable now flickers uncertainly between the pressures of job, home, and maybe even children. In this environment, the resolve to make a physical connection every day, without fail, for a whole month becomes more than just a healing measure; it becomes a dynamic act of reclamation.

The initial days may feel forced or awkward, like the cautious steps one takes in an unknown land. It makes sense. After all, the true meaning of intimacy is being willing to be open, curious, and accepting of one another at all times rather than in unrelenting perfection. These are the first interactions in which nonverbal communication takes shape, and touch, gaze, and emotion become powerful means of expression.

The daily ritual of making love becomes more than just a chore to be completed; it becomes a treasured moment. The pair begins to pick up on rhythms they had never noticed before; a glance, a touch, a grin take on new significance. They discover that intimacy is about more than just the physical act—it's also about the moments of calm after an embrace, shared vulnerability, and desire-laced laughter.

Take Lena and Sam's case, for example. They thought that their connection was becoming dimmer after eight years of marriage due to routine. Their pivotal moment came from this challenge. Though initially dubious, they discovered that putting their physical connection first opened the door to talking about deeper emotional wants and desires that had been hidden beneath years of routine. Every day's encounters woven together into a more intricate web of compassion and understanding changed their evenings and days.

That's not to imply there aren't any obstacles on the way. Stress, exhaustion, and unforeseen turns in life can seem unachievable. However, because of these challenges, the choice to go on and pick each other over again every day takes on a profoundly meaningful significance. It's a confirmation of the strength and profundity of the marital tie.

Additionally, this project might serve as a creative and exploratory playground. It's a call to break free from the constraints of daily life, to explore and find new opportunities for enjoyment and connection. The range of exploration is endless, from experimenting with different positions to adding aspects of play and surprise.

As the month ends, what's left is a transformed foundation rather than just a collection of experiences. Couples frequently describe feeling more appreciative of one another, having a stronger emotional bond, and having a renewed enthusiasm for life and their partner. It's a reminder that in the never-ending dance of life, being in step with your partner demands intention, work, and an open heart, and it's a reawakening to the power of physical proximity as a conduit for emotional connection.

By setting out on this adventure, newlyweds, eager learners, and seasoned spouses stand to uncover not just each other but also previously undiscovered facets of themselves. This is evidence for the theory that every lasting relationship has an unending reservoir of knowledge ready to be explored, provided one has the guts to do so.

While coaching clients, I frequently encourage them to get out of their calendars since the way we manage and react to our time has a significant impact on all aspects of our lives, including our relationships with others.
Husbands are included in this category. You will see a natural improvement in your marriage when you routinely make time for your significant other.
Over the course of the last year, I began color-coding my calendar so that I could see at a glance how well I was managing my time and whether I was living according to my principles. It's important to me that I have a fair quantity of brilliant Kelly-green appointments on my calendar each week, including one full day each week filled out as a "no plan zone," when my husband and I are both off from work.

This day represents my dedication to spending quality time with you and having a good time together. Visual clues on my calendar each week, such as an appointment and a color that corresponds to my heart chakra, serve as a constant reminder that my marriage is important to me and that it is something to be honored on anniversaries rather than something to be done on a daily basis.

And feel free to let go of any stress you may be feeling right now. It is not necessary for everything to run well every week. The pursuit of perfection is not the aim. Progress is being made.

Have sex every day for a month

If you haven't heard of "Sexy September," now is the time to Google it. I'm going to wait. On second thought, I'll save you the embarrassment and the tension by omitting the embarrassing search history.

Sexy September is exactly what the name suggests: a mutual and consensual commitment between you and your partner to have sex for 30 consecutive days in September. If you will, consider it a marathon of physical closeness.
The concept of having sex for 30 days straight may appear simple to one person and difficult to another, even to two people married to one another. To overcome this obstacle, commitment, creativity, and communication are required. And it can feel like a pain at times (even if you believe your partner is smokin' hot).

Therefore, why do it? To be honest, I believe that how you do one thing is how you do everything.

Therefore, if you are going to practice dedication, creativity, and communication with your husband in the bedroom, this experience will manifest itself in other areas of your life as well.
This will be really useful when it comes time to discuss last month's credit card bills or how you're going to handle the holidays this year.

So, do you have to wait until September to begin your rolling around? Certainly not. I say ignore Pope Gregory and his calendar if you choose to begin now.
The most critical aspect is to remain receptive to learning new things about your husband, yourself, and your marriage.

 Hear this, don't meditate to get good at mediation, but meditate to get good at life."
And I believe that the same principle applies here. You don't participate in Sexy September to improve your sex-sharing skills; instead, you participate in Sexy September to improve your life-sharing skills!

Learn a new language

I was given a basket full of delicacies by my bridesmaids after I was married, all of which they thought would be essential for my new life as a wife in the future. There was "a book that contains love languages," which was tucked in with the lovely robe, monogrammed wine glasses, and a cookbook. It took me one sitting to finish it, and I even persuaded my spouse to read it with me.

In the book, the author describes how each of us offers and receives emotional love in a relationship in a unique way, depending on our personalities.

The love languages" are "Words of Affirmation," "Quality Time," "Receiving Gifts," "Acts of Service," and "Physical Touch."

Following our reading of the book, we took a brief exam to determine our primary love languages, and we created "cheat sheets" to assist us in identifying the most meaningful methods to show our affection to one another.

Example: If your primary love language is "Actions of Service," you might find that your husband takes out the garbage and recyclables on a regular basis and include that on your list of things to be grateful for. However, if your primary love language is "Quality Time," it's likely that you'd rather he leave the garbage can where it is and come sit with you on the couch for some discussion and cuddling instead of taking the garbage out.

In the event that your spouse does not speak your major love language, or if he did not grow up in a household where love was conveyed in that manner, he may feel uncomfortable with the language you accept love in. If this is the case, I urge that you be patient with your husband, since it may appear that he is learning a foreign language.

I also started asking my husband how he felt about me on a scale of 1-10, and he responded positively. According to the author, you should ask your partner "how full their love tank is." Several times a month, I like to ask my spouse this question, and if he responds with a number lower than 8, I ask him what I can do to raise the number to at least a 10.

And if his number is at the higher end of the scale, I inquire as to why, so that I can continue to improve my ability to communicate in his language more fluently.

Chapter Summary

The creative idea of improving marital intimacy and understanding through colour-coding in calendars. It highlights the significance of setting aside deliberate time for one's spouse by introducing the concept with a potent metaphor about values appearing in one's bank account and calendar. The story looks at how committing to everyday sexual intercourse for a month may change people. It also discusses the importance of knowing and using your partner's preferred language for communication. Real-world examples are used to highlight the advantages of this practice. The chapter offers useful guidance, including original ideas for resolving conflicts and fortifying the marriage.

Important Points

Time Management Intentionality: Color-coding your calendar to prioritise spending time with your partner represents a conscious decision to cherish and strengthen your marriage.

The Power of Daily Intimacy: Having sex every day for a month can help couples reconnect, communicate better, and reignite their affection for one another.

Overcoming Difficulties Together: We recognise that stress and tiredness are inevitable roadblocks, but we also stress the value of perseverance and daily decision-making together.

Discovery and Creativity: To find new dimensions of pleasure and connection in a sexual relationship, it is important to foster play, surprise, and discovery.

Knowing Your Partner's Love Language and Speaking It: Filling your partner's "love tank" and increasing emotional intimacy and understanding are made possible by learning and speaking your partner's love language.

Important Takeaways

Marriage as a Dynamic Journey: The chapter emphasises marriage as an ongoing process of development, discovery, and strengthening bonds in which deliberate acts can result in significant advancements.

Sexuality as a Form of Communication: It is said that engaging in sexual activity is a rich kind of communication that conveys love, desire, and vulnerability in addition to being a physical act.

The Importance of Routine and Ritual: Creating routines that include daily intimacy or particular ways to spend time together can establish a framework for continued exploration and connection.

The Value of Adaptability: Despite life's unpredictability, intimacy and connection can only be sustained by the capacity to adjust and devise innovative solutions to problems.

Personal Development via Partnership: The shared commitment to pursuing intimacy and learning each other's love languages fosters a greater sense of camaraderie and personal progress.

Practical Exercises

Use Color-Coding to Build Connections: Set up a system on your calendar where a certain colour denotes time set aside for your spouse. Consider how your relationship is prioritised by this graphic aid.

Daily Intimacy Challenge: Make a monthly commitment to engaging in sexual intimacy every day and record the changes that occur in your relationship, communication, and emotional bond over time.

Love Language Discovery: Discuss how to better communicate love in each other's language, read a book on love languages together, then take the quiz to determine your primary love languages.

Overcoming Obstacles Discussion: Have an honest discussion about possible obstacles to regular intimacy and come up with original ideas for ways to keep the relationship going.

Exercise in Gratitude and Appreciation: For a month, keep a daily journal in which you record modest gestures or intimate moments with your relationship that you find meaningful. Pay particular attention to details pertaining to your partner's and your own love languages.

Reflection Time

In what ways does your present time management style demonstrate how much you value your marriage?

___
___
___
___
___
___
___
___
___
___
___
___
___
___
___

How can non-physical gestures of intimacy regularly strengthen your bond with your partner?

What can you learn from the difficulties and barriers you face when attempting daily intimacy? How do they resemble other elements of your relationship?

How has discovering intimacy and each other's love language helped you learn new things about each other and yourself?

_____
_____
_____
_____
_____
_____
_____
_____
_____
_____
_____
_____
_____
_____

Considering the habit of replenishing your significant other's "love tank," what better ways can you express your love in daily interactions?

_____
_____
_____
_____
_____
_____
_____
_____
_____
_____
_____
_____
_____
_____

CHAPTER FIVE

Have The Determination to Maintain a Cheerful State of Mind When Married

AS A WIFE FOR THE PAST 8 YEARS, I'VE CERTAINLY SEEN MY SHARE OF UPS and downs in my relationship with my husband. The overall point to remember is that no two marriages are same, and there is no such thing as a perfect **marriage that exists** in this world.

The only thing that matters is how satisfied both partners are with their marriage. And that happiness is not going to be the same from one day to the next. Some days are more pleasant than others, while other days may be particularly frustrating, as if they were the first time.

The most important thing is to have the motivation to maintain a joyful state of mind when you are married. The following are three areas of concentration that can assist in achieving or maintaining a positive frame of mind:

Self-awareness

The first and most important step toward becoming a better wife is to become more self-aware. It's critical to understand what makes you happy, as well as what you anticipate and desire from your partner, before you can start a relationship. Understanding yourself, as well as your strengths and weaknesses, is essential.

For example, if your partner has a tendency that you find bothersome, it is beneficial to understand how and why that habit affects you. There has to be an alternative course of action that will make you happy without having to urge your spouse to change his or her behavior. Or is there a solution that you and your partner can agree on that will alleviate the situation?

Self-awareness is the lighthouse that leads a person through the complex dance of marriage. It's not just about knowing oneself; it's also about looking deep within to see one's feelings, responses, and innermost thoughts to piece together the fabric of a relationship that depends on sincere understanding and connection.

Consider Sarah and Tom, who had just celebrated their fifth anniversary together. Their tale is one of laughter, love, and married life's natural ups and downs. However, hidden beneath their everyday pleasures and struggles lay unexplored regions of their inner selves waiting to be discovered. Tom, a passionate teacher, and Sarah, a committed nurse, became mired in their daily routines and frequently lost sight of the importance of genuinely knowing one another.

One night, while seated across from one another at their small dining table, a minor disagreement broke out about the forgotten task of emptying the garbage. But this had little to do with the rubbish; it was an outward sign of more profound, unspoken emotions. It was crucial for Sarah, who paused and inhaled deeply throughout their intense conversation. She recognised that this had nothing to do with proving a point or winning an argument. It was about realising why she had responded so strongly emotionally to this seemingly insignificant error.

Sarah had not known she was harbouring the underlying sensation of being taken advantage of until this moment of reflection. Acquiring self-awareness in their marriage commenced with this insight. It wasn't an easy road; perseverance, bravery, and the readiness to face hard facts were necessary. However, it was an essential one.

For Sarah and Tom, personal introspection and candid dialogue were the first steps towards developing self-awareness. They began setting aside time once a week to talk about their emotions, worries, and desires in an accepting and nonjudgmental environment. The goal of this exercise was to comprehend one another's viewpoints and emotional landscapes rather than to place blame.

Through this process, they learned the value of empathy and how a deeper awareness of oneself might lead to a deeper connection with others. Sarah discovered that her early years, when her accomplishments were frequently disregarded, were the root of her need for recognition and gratitude. Tom learned that a fear of confrontation caused his reluctance to disagree during family situations.

They set off on a voyage of self-discovery together, which strengthened their marriage despite life's turbulence and enhanced their love. It demonstrated that developing self-awareness is an ongoing process of learning and development rather than a final goal.

Self-awareness development is like taking care of a garden, particularly in relationships. It needs continual love, care, and attention. It's important to acknowledge that every partner is a person with distinct ideas, emotions, and life experiences. It's about realising these distinctions are not roadblocks but chances for development, education, and closer relationships.

As we manoeuvre through the intricate dynamics of matrimony, let us remember the tale of Sarah and Tom. Let it serve as a reminder that the basis of a solid, long-lasting relationship is the willingness to look within, gain self-awareness, and make room for unconditional love to blossom. This, my dear readers, is the core of self-awareness in marriage: a journey towards one's partner's heart and a self-understanding, resulting in an enduring and genuinely rewarding bond.

Flexibility

Life is a journey, and a long-lasting marriage is no exception. If you and your partner are in it for the long term, evolution will only be natural. It is critical to recognize that individuals change, that circumstances change, and that the dynamics of the relationship change as well.

As a result of all of the changes, it is critical that both sides be adaptable and have greater empathy towards one another. Empathy will aid in the creation of understanding, which will result in a deeper level of connection.

Being flexible in a marriage is like watching beautiful leaves dance in the wind; it's about dancing in unison even when the wind gusts aren't predicted. The key to flexibility is to adjust to changes in a way that improves your life and your spouse's, not to the point where you lose your shape. This principle, my dear readers, is particularly important for recently married couples, eager learners, seasoned spouses, and anybody looking to strengthen their relationship.

Let's imagine Sarah and Alex have been married for five years. Their trip serves as a wonderful example of flexibility. While Alex flourishes in the erratic world of event management, Sarah, a dedicated teacher, takes joy in the steady rhythm of the academic year. Instead of being a point of dispute, their disparate occupations serve as an example of the value of adaptability.

Sarah remembers an evening when Alex had to attend a critical function on their anniversary due to work obligations. At first, disillusionment casts a shadow over her heart. She welcomed change and regarded this as a chance rather than a setback. Sarah surprised Alex by planning a modest, private celebration at home the day before instead of insisting on celebrating on the actual day. This act of flexibility and understanding not only saved the day but also strengthened their relationship by showing them that their shared link mattered on their anniversary, regardless of the date.

In a marriage, being flexible also entails accepting each other's development and evolution. Think about Thomas and Evelyn, who had similar goals and desires when they married. Thomas's initial profession in banking was very different from the field of environmental conservation, which he found to be his new love over time. Evelyn supported Thomas in following his passion despite the uncertainty it offered since she saw the light in his eyes whenever he talked about his new interest. Their lives had to change due to this turnabout, from daily schedules to finances, but Evelyn's adaptability made their marriage work through all of these changes.

Being flexible in communication entails paying attention to understanding and reacting. It's about accepting your partner's viewpoints and emotions as legitimate, even though they may not align with yours. Imagine Lucy and Mark, who found out early in their marriage that their approaches to resolving conflicts were dissimilar. Mark needed time to gather his thoughts, but Lucy desired to discuss differences immediately. Rather than imposing their inherent inclinations on one another, they devised a tactic known as the "cool-off" interval. This strategy showed adaptability by giving Lucy the conversation she desired and Mark the room he needed.

These tales permeate with a deep understanding that flexibility does not need to sacrifice one's morals or happiness to maintain peace. Instead, the marriage is strengthened by a dynamic interplay of reciprocal bending and give-and-take. Similar to the foundation of a long-standing tree, adaptability enables a marriage to weather life's storms by swaying together rather than standing steady.

To all of the newlyweds, eager learners, seasoned spouses, and relationship enhancers who are reading this: see flexibility as a gift you can give each other rather than a compromise. It's the admission that your relationship is a dynamic, living creature that must be flexible to survive. Accept the erratic dance of marriage with grace and openness, and observe as it transforms into a lovely path of mutual development and unwavering love.

Communication

Too often in life, disagreements in a relationship emerge as a result of a breakdown in communication. To have a happy marriage, active communication is the most important skill to learn and practice throughout the partnership.

Do not assume that your partner is aware of what is going on in your head or what is upsetting you.

Just because you've been in a relationship with someone for a lengthy period of time does not necessarily imply that they are an expert on you or your situation. Be generous in your sharing of ideas, and be open-minded to others' as well.

In marriage, communication is a means of transportation and the cornerstone around which the union is constructed. Understanding sets the rhythm, and empathy directs the steps in this intricate dance of ideas, feelings, and wants. In this chapter, we explore the nuances of good communication, a skill that, when developed, weaves a rich tapestry of reciprocal respect and shared experiences into the marriage.

Consider the following situation, typical for many couples: Tom and Sarah, a recently married couple, became mired in miscommunication. Tom came home from a demanding and exhausting workday, wanting a peaceful evening. Full of joy about her recent promotion, Sarah waited for Tom to get back so she could tell Tom about it. But when he finally arrived, he was so tired that his answers were short and aloof. Sarah was stung, her happiness tempered by a pall of apparent apathy as she mistook his weariness for indifference.

Even in the cases of the most loving couples, communication can break down for the simple reason this scenario captures. It's essential to recognise the emotional undertones of our words in addition to just communicating information. According to Sarah and Tom, the core of the problem was different from what was said but rather the feelings and expectations that each party had brought to the discussion.

In a married relationship, good communication involves more than just talking; it also involves empathy, active listening, and a readiness to see things from your spouse's perspective. It's about realising that every discussion is an opportunity to deepen your relationship and add to the story of your shared existence. When confronted with obstacles, always remember that understanding and being understood are more important than winning a debate.

Think about "active listening," which is crucial for accomplishing meaningful conversation. It entails listening with all of your senses—not just hearing what is being said but also taking note of the tone, pauses, and emotions being kept silent. Sarah acted curiously, not accusingly, when she went up to Tom later to tell him how his previous answers had made her feel. This time, seeing his mistake, Tom expressed his fatigue and, in return, listened to Sarah's news with excitement and sincere curiosity. They avoided a possible confrontation by actively listening to one other, instead discovering a time of understanding and connection.

Being flexible in communication is crucial as it accommodates your partner's emotional state and the conversation's context. There are occasions when being direct is appropriate, times when being compassionate is appropriate, times when words are necessary to break the silence, and times when silence speaks louder than words.

Developing a common language that changes and develops with your marriage is the foundation of effective communication in a married couple. It's about learning to express love with a look, a touch, or a small deed of kindness and discovering beauty in the ordinary. It's about being determined to keep a positive outlook despite the unavoidable difficulties life throws at you. This common language becomes your haven, where you are respected, acknowledged, and seen.

Remember that communication skills lie at the core of each successful partnership as we negotiate the challenges of marriage. It is the bonding agent, the guiding light, and the base upon which love is erected and reconstructed daily. Let us learn to be

Samantha Nunez Chapman

both graceful dancers and watchful partners in this life dance, for it is in our mutual steps that we discover our rhythm and, in the end, our harmony.

Chapter Summary

In "Have The Determination to Maintain a Cheerful State of Mind When Married," the story explores the vital elements of developing a good mindset in a marriage, emphasising communication, self-awareness, and flexibility. Full of real-life examples and helpful suggestions, this chapter walks married people, particularly wives, through self-reflection, adjustment, and fulfilling communication. It highlights how crucial it is to have self-awareness, be receptive to change, and actively participate in sincere communication to cultivate a caring, encouraging, and strong marriage.

Important Points

Awareness of Oneself as the Basis: For personal development and a happy partnership, it is critical to acknowledge one's feelings, wants, and expectations. People who are self-aware are better equipped to comprehend and empathise with each other when navigating the challenges of marriage.

Embracing Flexibility: It's essential to be able to adjust to changes and accept how your spouse and relationship are changing. When flexibility and empathy are combined, a closer bond and stronger connection result.

The Importance of Communication: A happy marriage is built on effective communication. Emotional connection and mutual understanding depend on candid idea sharing and attentive listening.

Understanding and Empathy: Having a strong sense of empathy enables partners to respect one another's viewpoints and creates a loving atmosphere where respect and love can grow.

Cultivating a Joyful State of Mind: It's important to keep a cheerful mindset despite any difficulties that marriage may bring. A positive attitude improves the connection and fosters happiness and fulfilment.

Important Takeaways

Self-awareness Promotes Mutual Understanding: A better understanding of oneself can lead to a more compassionate and satisfying relationship.

Flexibility Builds a Stronger Marital Bond: Resilience and unity in marriage are fostered by the capacity to adjust to changes in life and your partner's development.

Communication is Multidimensional: It improves relationships between partners by involving listening, empathy, non-verbal clues, and spoken exchanges.

The Secret to Resolving Conflicts is Empathy: Potential disagreements can be turned into chances for development and closer relationships by learning to see the world from your partner's perspective.

A Happy Attitude Spreads: Maintaining a positive outlook on life helps the individual and spreads to their spouse, improving the quality of their marriage as a whole.

Practical Exercises

Daily Gratitude Journal: To promote appreciation and a good mindset, each spouse lists three things about the other daily.

Self-Reflection Sessions: To promote self-awareness and understanding between partners, set aside some time each week for introspection on one's thoughts, feelings, and behaviours. Then, share these insights with your partner.

Flexibility Challenges: Create situations in which one partner must adjust to a change that wasn't anticipated by the other to build empathy and flexibility in the relationship.

Engage in an Active Listening Role-Play: In this activity, two people communicate something meaningful to each other. In contrast, the other person listens intently and empathises without interjecting or providing advice.

Play activities that need nonverbal communication, like charades, to improve comprehension of one another's nonverbal signs and strengthen your emotional bond.

Reflection Time

How much do I know about my needs and wants, and how do they affect how I act with my partner?

_____
_____
_____
_____
_____
_____
_____
_____
_____
_____
_____
_____
_____

How can I show that I'm flexible enough to adjust to my partner's changing circumstances, and how can I be more flexible?

_____
_____
_____

Samantha Nunez Chapman

Do I engage in active listening in our regular conversations? If not, how can I improve it?

How can I approach arguments with greater understanding and empathy, and how can I respond to conflict?

What steps can I take to promote a happier and more optimistic mindset for myself and my marriage?

CHAPTER SIX

Soften your startup

According to research, women who initiate dialogues without expressing strong negativity are less likely to end up in a divorce.

WHEN TWO SEPARATE STREAMS OF THOUGHT AND EMOTION COME TOGETHER in marriage, the quality of the communication between them frequently determines how fertile the union will be. Softening one's tone in conversations—especially when viewed through the lens of maintaining a balance between positive and negative remarks—is one of the most important strategies for guaranteeing this fecundity. Understanding this subtle approach's significant influence on maintaining a happy, healthy marriage is important before delving into it.

Take the story of Elizabeth and James, a couple that used love as their compass when they started their marriage. But when reality set in, day-to-day struggles started to strain their relationship. With her enthusiasm as a beacon, Elizabeth frequently found herself giving more criticism than praise. The tides started to turn once they learned to offer five complimentary, grateful, and affirming statements for every unfavourable one.

Elizabeth heeded this counsel. She started each day by mentioning the little deeds James had done but had never received credit for. A soothing cup of tea placed on the nightstand, his deft handling of the clothes, or simply his understanding listening following her demanding workdays. When spoken, each gratitude served as a gentle salve for their strained relationships. With each passing moment, the positive energy that now permeated their interactions strengthened the strands of their relationship.

This method requires a change in viewpoint and acute awareness in practice. Every criticism or modification suggestion needs to be preceded by five affirmations. This does not imply putting off dealing with pressing matters. It's important to frame things in a context that emphasises and values the positive instead of the negative.

Consider the occasion when Elizabeth thought James was working excessively long hours. Rather than start with a criticism, she thanked him for his commitment to supporting their family, complimented his work ethic, acknowledged his assistance with her job, remembered a recent act of love he had done, and thanked him for his efforts in keeping their house in good condition. Only then did she softly mention how much she missed his company and wanted to spend more time with him.

This method, which has its roots in the psychology of positive reinforcement, emphasises the importance of people recognising and valuing each other in interpersonal relationships. Couples like Elizabeth and James foster a loving atmosphere where love can blossom despite difficulties by prioritising encouraging words. Changing the emphasis from what is lacking to the abundance present in the relationship promotes an attitude of appreciation and respect for one another.

Whether you are a newlywed pair, a motivated learner, an experienced spouse, or someone looking to improve your relationship, applying this technique to everyday encounters can make a big difference in the quality of your bond. It serves as a reminder that although progress and understanding are attainable goals, perfection is an illusion. Leading with positivity can change the path into a rewarding journey of mutual discovery and strengthening love in the delicate dance of marriage, where every step counts.

So, let us remember the importance of words and their ability to deeply impact the core of our relationships as we negotiate the challenges of communicating in marriage. We soften our startups and fortify the basis of our affection by making a commitment to five nice comments for every negative one.. That is, complaining without blaming anyone, refraining from condemning the individual and sticking to the facts, and refraining from making judgments and evaluations. Use "I" instead of "you," and be mindful of your physiological and emotional reactions so that you can maintain your composure, politeness, respect, and appreciation.

Instead, of using sarcasm or ambiguous passive-aggressive statements, give specific instructions instead.

Give 5 positive, appreciative, grateful remarks for each 1 negative

Even if you're only thinking about it and not saying it out loud, do it. According to research, keeping a 5:1 ratio of positive contacts is beneficial not only for relationship success but also for the individual's overall well-being as well.

The secret to a happy marriage is balancing our expressions, especially in combining the positive and the bad. Offering five positive, grateful, or appreciative remarks for every negative comment is a technique I have discovered to be transforming. This strategy is more than a recommendation; when applied effectively, it may strengthen your bond and foster a deeper understanding.

Let us consider Laura and Aaron, who recently marked their second marriage anniversary. Being a quick learner at work, Sarah frequently carried her frustrations from the day into her home. Conversely, Aaron tended to reserve and inwardize his frustrations from his workday. Their evenings started to play out like a predetermined play: Laura would complain about her day while Aaron would listen silently until the atmosphere was heavy with unvoiced complaints.

The pivotal moment occurred when Laura, following an incredibly demanding day, began her typical rant, only to encounter an unexpected reply from Alex. He softly said, "I admire your passion for your work." "Your dedication to solving problems is something I've always respected." This was an acknowledgement of her spirit rather than a rejection of her emotions. Laura hesitated, surprised. The air changed. A warmth that had been absent from their recent exchanges replaced the tension that had been growing.

This incident powerfully reminds us of the effectiveness of positive reinforcement. By concentrating on Laura's advantages, Aaron made room for a more productive discussion. After that, they could address the drawbacks in a less hostile and encouraging setting. Finding this balance involves facing the problems with compassion and respect rather than avoiding them.

Practising the five-to-one ratio involves developing an appreciative mindset rather than maintaining a score. It's about identifying and expressing the tiny, sometimes missed actions that strengthen your relationship. Saying "thank you" for making the bed, "I appreciate your patience," or "I appreciate your effort to listen to your partner" could suffice.

Think about Jessica and John, who negotiated the challenges of merging their families in a different story. The difficulties were numerous, ranging from managing expectations to harmonising parenting philosophies. Friction resulted from Jessica's frequent criticism of John's more forgiving behaviour with the kids. Jessica changed her focus after realising how much stress this placed on their marriage. She thanked John for his generosity and ability to make the children laugh—even under stressful circumstances. She was grateful for his efforts to foster a sense of inclusion and belonging among all of them. This change in perspective calmed their exchanges and increased Jessica's openness to John's points of view, encouraging a cooperative rather than combative approach to their problems.

The key to this idea is that it can build a solid emotional foundation in your connection. Every kind word serves as a deposit, creating a store of goodwill that can withstand the unavoidable withdrawals caused by critical remarks. It's about building a solid foundation that your marriage will withstand storms, as they will.

Incorporating this idea into your everyday interactions can change the dynamic of your relationship, whether you are a newlywed pair, an eager learner, an experienced spouse, or someone looking to better your relationship. Fostering an atmosphere of appreciation, acknowledgement, and respect for one another builds the foundation for a relationship that can withstand and prosper despite life's ups and downs.

To sum up, our marriages are a story that we write together, using the language we use, the gratitude we show, and the grace with which we resolve our differences. Adopting the principle of offering five compliments for every criticism does more than enhance communication; it also builds a marriage based on compassion, understanding, and an unbreakable pact of respect for one another.

Learn your own and your partner's love language

It is beneficial to know your love language as a couple to better translate loving gestures and avoid missing out on well-intentioned behaviors of connection to capture more opportunities for thankfulness.

The Five Love Languages has a profile for you that you may read about at their website. Gifts, quality time, acts of service, physical love, and words are all examples of expressions of affection. Having a good understanding of your partner's language allows you to express your affection in a way that they will recognize, and you can receive it knowing that their style may be different from yours.

Knowing the love languages of both you and your spouse can significantly change the dynamics of your marriage. It can serve as a lighthouse to help you navigate the challenges of emotional intimacy and connection. This understanding is fundamental to communicating love in a way that makes your acts of affection significant to your partner.

For a brief period, consider the tale of Eleanor and Theo, a couple who came to a dead end despite their intense love for one another. As a talented writer, Eleanor lavished Theo with poems and love letters, considering them the pinnacle of her affection. On the other hand, Theo wished Eleanor would show her love in ways that relieved his everyday difficulties, like cooking or helping with housework, as he felt most loved when he served others. Their conceptions of love and their actions were at odds, which caused them to feel neglected and undervalued. This unneeded conflict damaged their marriage.

The lightbulb moment arrived when Eleanor discovered the theory of love languages while trying to strengthen her marriage. She recognised that the secret to expressing her love to Theo in a way that he could genuinely feel it was to know and speak his love language. Their relationship underwent a complete transformation as a result of this discovery.

Gary Chapman identified five love languages: physical touch, acts of service, words of affirmation, getting gifts, and quality time. Finding out about oneself and one's partner's primary love language—which each individual has a deeper connection to than others—can be an enlightening experience.

Think about the influence of affirmations in a marriage when one person gets their energy from hearing others express their love and gratitude. Saying something as simple as "I'm proud of you" or "I appreciate all you do for us" can go a long way towards boosting their sense of accomplishment and worth.

In contrast, acts of service are the best way to demonstrate the saying "actions speak louder than words" to people who understand love through modest but meaningful deeds. These small gestures of kindness, like replacing the children's morning routines or repairing a leaky tap, express gratitude and affection.

Receiving gifts is a sign of attention and effort rather than consumerism, and it is considered a love language. Unexpected gifts, no matter how big or expensive, are a potent way to show someone you care about them even when you're not around.

Devoted and unbroken time spent together is a love language beyond physical proximity. It entails actively interacting and building a connection with one's spouse to give their time together purpose and fulfilment.

Finally, for some people, physical touch is the primary way to express love and comfort. Love is more beautifully expressed by a tender touch, a cosy hug, or a comforting hand squeeze than it can be through words.

Knowing these love languages can open doors to deeper, more satisfying relationships for engaged couples, seasoned spouses, and aspirant learners. It involves stepping outside our comfort zones and putting ourselves in our partners' shoes to customise our displays of love to meet their most basic emotional requirements.

In summary, discovering your and your partner's love languages is a journey that will help you strengthen the closeness and connection that are the cornerstones of your marriage, not just your communication skills. This knowledge ensures a long-lasting, loving union by fostering an atmosphere where love flourishes, minimises misunderstandings, and strengthens the marital tie.

Chapter Summary

"Soften Your Startup," discusses the need to start marital conversations constructively. It explores the need to maintain a 5:1 ratio of positive to negative encounters and the efficacy of balancing positive and negative statements. It shows how easing the start of talks creates a healthier, more loving, and supportive relationship through the real-life stories of couples like Elizabeth, James, Laura and Aaron. The story also presents the idea of love languages to improve comprehension and intimacy in the marriage, providing a whole manual for fostering a happy union via considerate dialogue and expressions of gratitude.

Important Points

Starting a Positive Dialogue: Women who initiate talks without negativity are less likely to divorce, emphasising how crucial dialogue starting is for the stability of marriages.

The 5:1 Positive to Negative Ratio states that providing five positive remarks for every critical or negative one can greatly enhance the atmosphere of your relationship and build a deeper, more loving bond.

Real-life Applications: The chapter uses the stories of couples like Elizabeth and James to show how a 5:1 ratio and gentler discussion starters might improve a tense relationship.

The Psychology of Positive Reinforcement: Highlighting the good things in your partner and your relationship creates an atmosphere conducive to love and gratitude, which helps couples get through difficult times.

Understanding Love Languages: It's essential to be aware of and considerate of each other's love languages to properly translate loving gestures, prevent miscommunication, and strengthen emotional bonds.

Important Takeaways

The Function of Communication in Marital Health: Effective communication has a critical role in the health of a marriage, with positive beginnings serving as a spark for a deeper level of understanding and bonding.

Balance of Positive and Negative Interactions: Creating an atmosphere where both partners feel respected and understood is more important than avoiding disagreements when it comes to balancing positive and negative remarks.

The Relationship Dynamic Can Be Changed by Consistently Expressing Gratitude and Appreciation: Mutual respect and love can be strengthened when gratitude and appreciation are given regularly.

Positive Reinforcement in Action: Stressing the positive aspects of a marriage instead of concentrating on its flaws fosters a culture of acceptance and validation, which is necessary for emotional satisfaction.

Tailoring Love Expressions: By learning and using your partner's preferred language, you can establish deeper relationships and make sure that your actions of love are appreciated and acknowledged.

Practical Exercises

Every day, each couple should write down five things they value about the other, and after the week, they should share their daily gratitude logs.

The 5:1 Challenge: Intentionally use a 5:1 ratio of positive to negative remarks for a week in your conversations. Observe any changes in the dynamics of your relationships.

Love Languages Discovery: After taking the Love Languages quiz together, discuss how to express love more effectively in your partner's native tongue.

Positive Startups Practice: Act out dialogues on difficult subjects, emphasising the importance of accepting one another's viewpoints and positively starting the conversation.

Appreciation Jar: Make an appreciation jar to place your positive remarks and letters of gratitude. Distribute these notes once a week at a specified time.

Reflection Time

How do you usually start a conversation with your spouse about tough subjects, and how does that affect the result?

_____
_____
_____
_____
_____
_____
_____
_____
_____
_____
_____
_____
_____

Think back to a recent disagreement or miscommunication. Would the course of that talk have been different if the 5:1 ratio had been used?

_____
_____
_____

How often do you see your significant other using their primary love language to show their affection? What reaction have you had to it?

Think back to a moment when your partner showed you how much they valued you. How did you feel about them and the relationship resulting from what they said or did?

How can you improve your emotional intimacy and connection by implementing your knowledge of each other's love languages into your everyday interactions?

CHAPTER SEVEN

Use the K.N.O.W. Method

How to enhance your marriage and become a better wife using the K.N.O.W method: four steps to success!

#1 Decide what kind of wife you want to be

AS A WIFE, THERE IS NO SUCH THING AS A PRE-DEFINED ROLE BECAUSE you are constantly expanding and growing. I realized early in my marriage that I needed to figure out what kind of wife I wanted to be based on my abilities, weaknesses, desires, and my family's requirements.

Because it was different from how I started as a wife, it took bravery for me to choose and modify my role as a wife. My marriage improved and allowed me to better connect with my spouse when I totally embraced the shift, despite how difficult it was at first.

Determining the type of wife, you want to be is a crucial step towards the adventure of marriage. This question reveals a person's deepest beliefs, aspirations, and expectations when considered carefully. The K.N.O.W. approach, especially the first key, "Know what kind of wife you want to be," acts as a compass to help you navigate the complex web of duties and responsibilities with marriage.

Consider, for example, a situation in which Emma, a committed worker and recent bride, is faced with a decision. Her heart longs for a peaceful and supportive home life, but her profession requires long hours and steadfast dedication. Her conflicting desires put her in a difficult situation that many people encounter. Emma's narrative is not exceptional; rather, it represents the contemporary wife who must strike a balance between her own goals and the well-being of her marriage.

Choosing what kind of wife you want to be is a lifelong process impacted by the changing phases of a marriage rather than a single thought. Your job as a wife changes to suit your partner's needs and goals, regardless of whether you are newlyweds, deep in the thick of parenting experiences, or rediscovering each other in your golden years.

Think of Lucy, who chose to embark on a path of self-exploration and rejuvenation following her silver wedding anniversary. She reflected on her years as a spouse, a friend, and a carer and realised how crucial it is to be a woman who puts her personal development and happiness first. Her choice to continue her education boosted her self-esteem and provided a new life to her marriage. Lucy's tale reinforces the idea that being a good wife also entails taking care of yourself and encouraging personal development in tandem with relationship improvement.

And there's the story of Aisha and Tom, whose union served as a living example of the strength of flexibility and support among one another. Tom, a reserved scholar, and Aisha, a lively soul who loved social work, derived strength from their differences. Aisha and her spouse established a foundation to assist poor kids due to Aisha's choice to be a wife who ardently supports her partner's aspirations and her own. Their experience demonstrates how being a wife encompasses more than just staying at home; it also involves working together to attain goals and realise shared aspirations.

With its focus on self-awareness and clarity, the K.N.O.W. technique invites you to consider the sort of wife you want to be and the kind of person you want to become inside the marriage. It all comes down to realising that marriage is a union of equals in which both partners support one another while having the freedom to develop, dream, and be who they are.

By using this approach, you're not just taking on a job but setting out on a path of introspection and exploration with others. It's a dedication to creating an environment where both partners flourish—not just as spouses but also as people. The narratives of Emma, Lucy, and Aisha provide striking examples of how a person might understand and carry out the role of a wife; they also serve as a lighthouse for individuals attempting to negotiate the challenges of married life.

Aside from being a very personal choice, deciding what kind of wife you want to be also expresses your vision for your future together. It's a call to conversation, common goals, and a relationship that develops and changes with time. As you explore this issue, think about the values most important to you and your partner, your ambitions for the future, and the legacy you hope to leave behind. Doing this sets the stage for a long-lasting, fulfilling, and enriching marriage.

#2 No. The word "no" is a complete sentence in and of itself.

Wives must learn to say no when the situation calls for it. It is easy to become a husband-pleaser and lose yourself in the process of always feeling obligated to say "yes," when the proper response should be a polite "no."
That, on the other hand, is the quickest way to become burned out, bitter, and resentful of others. The ability to set boundaries and enforce those boundaries can assist you in becoming a more content wife.

While communication has unmatched power, its most profound essence in marriage frequently resides in its simplicity. The power of a single word, "No," stands out among the many ways to express oneself; it is a testament to the clarity and respect essential for a successful partnership. This section explores the skill of saying "No" in a married setting, emphasising how important it is for engaged couples and more experienced partners.

Take time to read the story of Ella and Jamie, a couple who perfectly embodies the need for mutual respect and understanding in communication. In the early days of their marriage, Ella was inundated with requests and invites, not only from Jamie but also from friends and other family members. She stretched herself too thin, risking her health and their relationship out of a desire to please and a dread of disappointment.

Ella's discovery that 'No' is a complete sentence and the K.N.O.W. approach marked a turning point in her life. At first, she was concerned that saying "No" could plant seeds of dissatisfaction or bitterness. But she also learned that saying "no" may bridge tremendous respect and understanding between people when said with love and respect.

Jamie was relieved and impressed by Ella's newly discovered assertiveness rather than frustrated. He had taken her compliance for enthusiasm, not realising the weight of his expectations on her. Ella's ability to set limitations with a straightforward "No" sparked a conversation about shared obligations, priorities, and boundaries, giving their union a renewed sense of harmony and balance.

This story demonstrates that saying "no" is more than just a word; it's a communication tool that, when employed wisely, can strengthen a marriage. It encourages honest communication between partners about their needs, wants, and constraints, creating a space where everyone feels heard, appreciated, and valued.

Furthermore, 'No' promotes independence within a united partnership, reminding them that personal space and uniqueness are acceptable and necessary for a robust and happy marriage. It refutes the fallacy that unity necessitates homogeneity and promotes a partnership enhanced by difference and respect for one another.

Let's embrace the strength and simplicity of saying "no" as we negotiate the intricacies of married life. Let it serve as a reminder that genuine harmony in marriage, like in life, emerges from the presence of respect, understanding, and the guts to have open and honest communication rather than from the absence of conflict.

#3 Opportunities

Always be on the lookout for possibilities to create win-win scenarios for both you and your husband. The majority of individuals advise you to learn how to compromise in a relationship. Over time, you get bored and alienated from your desires and requirements since you have been compromising them.
Learning how to create win-win scenarios for both you and your husband will allow you to strengthen your marriage's relationship even more.

Opportunities are like secret threads in the large and complex variety of marriage; when sewn carefully, they may turn the fabric of your partnership into a work of resilience, strength, and beauty. Recognising opportunities in marriage entails appreciating minor moments and larger ones that can promote understanding, development, and a closer bond between you and your partner. It's about elevating the ordinary into the significant and the commonplace into the remarkable.

For a moment, let us imagine the tale of Ella and Sam, a couple enmeshed in the daily grind of existence. Their relationships had devolved into transactions as they balanced professional obligations and domestic duties, keeping their chats to the essentials. Ella stumbled onto an opportunity over a charred breakfast toast one calm Sunday morning. Instead of moaning over the burnt toast, she chuckled and pointed jokingly to Sam's captivating appeal from the previous evening. This brief, lighthearted time spent in jest began a day full of laughing, memories, and rediscovering their love for one another.

This story captures the spirit of making use of marriage's opportunities. It's not always about lavish presents or large gestures. More often than not, it's about the small details of everyday life—the choice to be kind instead of critical, to lend a helping hand when things become challenging, or to share a little laughter in the middle of the mayhem. Opportunities are when you choose to be your partner's ally instead of your enemy and choose compassion and love over apathy and annoyance.

Think about the opportunities that arise from obstacles or disputes. These aren't just challenges; they're opportunities for development. When confronted with disagreements, embracing a viewpoint that aims to comprehend before being understood and sympathising before anticipating empathy presents a chance to strengthen your relationship. It's about creating bridges where walls may have arisen and finding common ground even when viewpoints diverge.

It takes some attentiveness to engage with opportunities fully; you must try to be present in the moments you spend with your partner. It's about seeing, not only seeing, and listening, not just hearing. It's about losing yourself entirely in the experiences that you share, whether they be happy times, sad times, or just the peaceful quiet of friendship.

Furthermore, opportunities in marriage go beyond the exchanges you have with your partner. Among these are the opportunities you provide for yourself to develop personally. Whether via a hobby, work advancement, or improving your physical and mental health, personal growth enhances the unique elements you bring to your marriage. Growing yourself means bringing fresh views, energy, and life into your relationship; this creates a dynamic, ever-evolving partnership.

To all of you—newlyweds, eager learners, seasoned spouses, and relationship enhancers—remember that marriage is an infinitely fertile garden. Every day is filled with countless moments waiting to be turned into chances for development, love, and understanding. Grab hold of these moments and incorporate them into the very fabric of your partnership. By doing this, you improve as a spouse and jointly build a dynamic, long-lasting, and pleasing marriage.

#4 Wisdom

To have a successful marriage, it is necessary to be wise. A lady who demonstrates sound judgment in her speech and actions will win her husband's affection and respect.

So, here are my top three bits of advice that have had the most significant impact on my marriage:

The thread of awareness and foresight frequently shines the brightest in the fabric of marital wisdom. With wisdom as its last beacon, the K.N.O.W. approach functions like a lighthouse to help ships navigate stormy seas. Couples can find comfort and support in this area of wisdom, whether they are just starting together or navigating the rough waters of a long-term partnership.

In the context of marriage, wisdom goes beyond a simple understanding of the world or the accumulation of life's experiences. It represents the profound capacity to identify our partner's underlying needs, desires, and concerns. Wisdom is the result of striking a balance that promotes development, mutual respect, and understanding, as well as knowing when to talk, when to listen, and when to stand firm and concede.

Take the case of Eliza and Samuel, a couple who found themselves at a fork in the road after a few years of marriage. Like many others, they had experienced their fair share of hardships, but their wisdom helped them light their way ahead. Samuel had always been encouraged to communicate his emotions and worries by Eliza, who was a strong proponent of the benefits of honest communication. But her wisdom made her understand the importance of approach and timing. She became adept at seeing when Samuel was most open to her so that he would listen to her without closing his mouth when she spoke.

Samuel, on his part, demonstrated knowledge through deeds. He made a deliberate effort to do deeds of kindness that spoke to Eliza's heart because he knew that love is often expressed in small, commonplace gestures. These small gestures of kindness, like cooking her favorite dinner after a long day or pausing to see a sunset, greatly heightened their relationship.

Another sign of wisdom is the capacity to anticipate difficulties and take proactive measures to address them. For example, Eliza and Samuel decided not to allow the unavoidable tensions that come with financial strain to cause a rift between them.

Rather, they used their combined knowledge to create a plan that put their relationship first, willing to make concessions and sacrifices when needed but always keeping mutual understanding and support as the main objective.

Furthermore, wisdom in marriage entails accepting the idea of personal and joint development. It acknowledges that change is inevitable and that intelligence and foresight must adjust. It entails creating an atmosphere where both may flourish and accepting your spouse for who they are and who they are becoming.

To put it simply, wisdom holds the K.N.O.W. method's components together, ensuring that openness, knowledge, nurturing, and wisdom work together rather than separately. The cornerstone provides a foundation sturdy enough to endure the test of time to develop rewarding, long-lasting relationships.

Let wisdom be your compass if you're a newlywed pair, an eager student, an experienced spouse, or someone looking to strengthen your marriage. It's a process of ongoing education, comprehension, and, most importantly, love. May the insight you develop guide you as you weave your marriage tapestry, adding richness, happiness, and resiliency to your life together.

Chapter Summary

The K.N.O.W. method's transformational effectiveness in improving marriages and personal development in the context of being a better wife. It happens in four crucial steps:
- Choosing the kind of wife you want to be.
- Realising the value of saying "no."
- Taking advantage of chances for growth together.
- Using wisdom in both words and deeds.

With its practical examples and thoughtful advice, this approach is a lighthouse for ladies who want to strengthen their bond with their husbands, welcome personal growth, and cultivate a loving, supporting marriage.

Important Points

Self-reflection and Development: If you want to be the wife you want to be, you need to introspection to realise your needs and desires and how they fit into your family dynamics. It's a dynamic process of expansion and adaptation.

The Power of "No": Establishing healthy marital dynamics where both parties feel appreciated and respected requires the ability to say "no" with confidence. It also helps people maintain personal limits and avoid burnout.

Seizing Opportunities: By identifying and taking advantage of opportunities, a couple can strengthen their marriage by turning routine moments into opportunities for growth and connection.

Practical Wisdom: Practicing wisdom in a marriage means knowing your spouse's needs, deciding when to talk to them, and showing sincere kindness to foster respect and affection.

Holistic Approach: The K.N.O.W. technique promotes a holistic strategy for strengthening marriages, stressing the value of mutual support, honest communication, and personal development.

Important Takeaways

Marriage as a Changing Path: Being a better wife is a continuous process that reflects how both individual and shared life experiences change over a marriage.

Communication Nuances: Timing, delivery, and the capacity for active listening are all important aspects of good communication in a marriage, in addition to the content of what is stated.

Personal Development: Stressing that taking care of oneself is just as important as being a good wife, personal development and self-care are essential to the longevity of any marriage.

Flexibility and Support: A marriage is strong when the spouses can support one another's goals and objectives and work together to adjust to life's changes.

Wisdom as a Foundation: To build a strong, satisfying marriage, a couple must possess wisdom, which includes insight, comprehension, and the application of knowledge.

Practical Exercises

Thinking Back Write in your journal: Take a week to consider the kind of wife you want to be. Keep a journal where you discuss your marriage's needs and how your strengths and places for improvement connect.

Boundary Setting: To develop your confidence, start with simple, non-confrontational settings where you practise saying "no" to situations that make you feel overwhelmed or uncomfortable.

Opportunity Day: Set aside a day to actively look for and seize chances to spend quality time with your spouse, whether it be through hobbies, conversations, or physical affectionate gestures.

Acts of Wisdom: Pick one day a week to show your partner some consideration, acting on your knowledge of their preferences and requirements.

Marriage objectives Workshop: Hold a workshop with your spouse to discuss individual and joint objectives for your partnership. The session should centre on personal growth, communication, and support from one another.

Reflection Time

How can I improve my marriage by addressing the areas of my personal development that I have ignored since becoming a wife?

_____
_____
_____
_____
_____
_____
_____
_____
_____
_____
_____
_____
_____
_____

What does it tell about my communication style or worries, and how do I usually respond when I have to say "no" to my partner?

_____
_____
_____

Samantha Nunez Chapman

Is there a recent instance when I could have done more to strengthen my relationship with my spouse? How can I be more present going forward and offer apologies?

How have I exhibited wisdom in our marriage, and what more can I do to develop this trait?

When I think back on the K.N.O.W. approach, which area is the most difficult for me, and how can I get better at it?

CHAPTER EIGHT

Align your priorities with those of your Husband.

It's important to know where the other person is coming from when you have differences, and this brings more understanding in your communication.

LEARN WHAT THE MINOR STUFF IS, AND HOW NOT TO GET TOO WORKED UP ABOUT IT.
Men are typically brought up in a different manner than women, and as a result, they are less concerned with details such as whether all of the flatware on the table is from the same set.

This is not a big deal in the broad scheme of things, so instead of picking on him about it, just leave it go or buy only one type of silverware for the time being. Your life and marriage will be significantly improved if you recognize that he simply does not notice these types of nuances and that he is not acting carelessly in order to annoy you.

Please let him some breathing space and allow him to be himself.
Allow your husband to devote his attention to the things that are important to him in his life. You should let him to make decisions on his own, without you knowing every aspect of his plans — he isn't a toddler.

You should treat your husband as an independent adult, place some faith in his judgment, and acknowledge and respect his needs, even if you don't fully understand them. I assure you that he will be grateful.

In marriage, when two spirits unite to set out on a path full of thrilling and ordinary moments, there is a fine art to giving each other permission to be who they are. Despite its apparent simplicity, this idea significantly impacts the durability and quality of a marriage. Each partner's uniqueness is a thread that contributes color and texture to the shared life tapestry, enhancing the overall composition.

Consider the tale of Eliza and Thomas, a couple with dreams and love who entered the holy marriage union. As recentlyweds, they excitedly dissolved into each other's worlds, relishing the novelty of their union. However, as the months passed, the unrelenting blending of their lives started to erode the boundaries of their uniqueness. An enthusiastic painter, Eliza discovered that her easel was collecting dust, and Thomas's guitar was silent and had no strings on it. Their tale is an example of a typical marital mistake: the unintentional repression of one's individuality in the pursuit of unity.

This chapter explores the nuances of giving your spouse room to be himself—a notion that, despite appearing to be at odds with the ideals of marital unity, is one of its strongest proponents. Allowing your spouse to pursue his interests, pastimes, and friendships outside of the marriage is a significant show of love and respect, not a sign of disengagement. It recognizes his individuality and reaffirms your dedication to his wellbeing.

Practical counsel from the real world advises starting candid conversations about each other's interests, goals, and the small things that bring you joy. In addition to fostering understanding, this conversation lays the groundwork for a partnership in which both parties feel heard and respected. Recall that it's important to actively support each other's interests and social circles rather than just putting up with them. This may include supporting your spouse in going out with his buddies or taking up a new activity that doesn't involve you.

Furthermore, the story of another couple, Eleanor and Jacob, demonstrates the transformational potential of adopting this approach. Despite the latter being a nature lover, Eleanor didn't share Jacob's fondness for solo excursions in the forest.

Eleanor supported Jacob's solitary travels rather than constantly demanding to be at his side, realizing that these experiences were not merely diversions but vital to his wellbeing. In exchange, Eleanor received encouragement from Jacob, who frequently surprised her with books by well-known authors. Their narrative shows us that, ironically, when we give each other space, we give each other the gift of self-discovery and become closer.

Finding a balance to promote this culture of independence and respect for one another is essential. Giving someone space shouldn't turn into emotionally separating them. It's about preserving the warmth and intimacy of your relationship while letting your husband explore his uniqueness. Maintaining this balance can be facilitated by frequent check-ins, sharing experiences, and showing interest in each other's endeavors.

As we maneuver through the intricacies of matrimony, let us always remember that love, at its most basic, yields liberation. It gives us the confidence to be who we are, fearlessly and unapologetically, in front of another. You're supporting your husband's uniqueness and strengthening the basis of your marriage at the same time when you give him room to breathe and be himself. Love finds its fullest expression in this hallowed place of acceptance and understanding, and the marriage path serves as a monument to the beauty of separate yet united lives.

Through this investigation, we have explored the domain of individual autonomy within the marriage contract, revealing its importance in fostering a partnership built on sincerity and reciprocity. This chapter, using real-life examples and helpful tips, highlights how crucial it is to give your spouse the freedom to be himself to build a happy and satisfying marriage.

Chapter Summary

The crucial habit is recognising and permitting individuality in the marriage while setting priorities aligned with one's spouse. It emphasises how crucial it is to accept diversity and not worry about trivial things like mismatched cutlery, which are unimportant in the big picture. It emphasises the importance of giving your partner room to be themselves and shows how marriages are strengthened when partners recognise and value each other's independence.

Important Points

Acknowledging and honouring partners' disparities in upbringing and viewpoints can improve communication and foster a deeper level of understanding in the marriage.

Minor Stuff: Being able to tell important problems from little ones makes it easier to avoid becoming overly worked up over trivial matters, which promotes a calmer and more accepting home atmosphere.

Giving Space: Mutual respect and trust are strengthened in marriages when partners are free to follow their interests and make decisions.

Individuality in Unity: Preserving one's individuality within a married partnership enhances the partnership's dynamics and the shared life experience.

Encouraging Each Other's Interests: Showing love and respect for one another by actively encouraging and participating in each other's extramarital interests and pastimes strengthens the marriage.

Important Takeaways

Matrimony as an Equitable Partnership: In a marriage, valuing each other's uniqueness and independence fosters a more solid, equal alliance.

It's All About Communication: Understanding and respecting one another are based on having frank conversations about each other's needs, hobbies, and the little things in life that make us smile.

Disengagement Does Not Result from Independence: Not an indication of emotional separation, but a meaningful display of love and respect is allowing one's spouse to be themselves.

The Harmony between Unity and Uniqueness: A happy marriage requires striking a balance between providing support and granting personal development and discovery.

Love Sets Free: Being one's true self is made possible by true love, which infuses a depth of acceptance and understanding into marriages.

Practical Exercises

Make a "Joy List" by noting down the little things that make you happy on your own and sharing it with your partner to help them respect and value each other's uniqueness.

Arrange Your Own Activities: Allocate a specific amount of time for each couple to pursue their interests or hobbies on their own and then discuss the experiences together.

Dine Alone with Friends: To promote social relationships outside of marriage, encourage one another to go out to dine alone with friends.

Establish an 'Independence Day' every month: Set up a single day per month for each partner to explore their passions on their own, fostering trust and providing personal space.

Talk about and rearrange your priorities: Discuss your priorities together and individually over a meal, making sure that each spouse feels acknowledged and appreciated.

Reflection Time

What unique qualities about you have you felt compelled to conceal or alter in your marriage, and how can you get them back?

_____
_____
_____
_____
_____
_____
_____
_____
_____
_____
_____
_____
_____

How can you effectively explain your wants and interests to your spouse to ensure mutual respect and understanding?

_____
_____
_____
_____
_____
_____

Think back to a moment when allowing your partner some space improved your relationship. What insights did that experience give you?

How do you balance the desire to develop personally and the obligation to develop as a couple?

Samantha Nunez Chapman

How can you show your love and respect for your spouse's uniqueness by actively supporting their interests and activities different from yours?

CHAPTER NINE

Create a way of talking that everyone can understand and that makes them feel like they are being heard

As a way to avoid this, don't think your partner doesn't listen to or understand what you say. Instead of complaining, ask for what you want in concrete, clear, and measurable terms instead of just complaining about it.

If you think that "sex doesn't matter," think again. It really does

IF YOU USE SEX TO EXPRESS INTIMACY, IT'S A CRUCIAL AND HEALTHY ASPECT of a happy marriage. So be open and honest about your sexual preferences. Communication will enhance your experience and allow the connection you share outside of the bedroom to bloom into something you'll both love.

Regarding marriage, the importance of closeness and sex between spouses is a topic that is frequently discussed with a mixture of interest and caution. While many parts of a relationship revolve around it, it's typical to hear people minimize its significance by saying things like "Sex doesn't matter." But dig a little farther into the fabric of marriage relationships. You'll find a different story in which happiness and harmony between partners primarily depend on the physical tie.

Just picture a pair, Sarah and Tom, if you will. Even though they have been married for a year and are incredibly in love, they still have trouble discussing their shortcomings. Being physically apart has caused Sarah to ponder why their once-strong bond seems to be fading. However, Tom cannot pinpoint the reason for his growing distance. This situation occurs in many partnerships, highlighting an essential fact that is difficult to overlook: making love is more than just a physical act; it is a profound form of communication that expresses much more than words can.

This chapter explores this complex dance of intimacy and shows how it's about developing a deeper understanding, mutual respect, and connection rather than just meeting a biological need. It involves declaring, "I see you, I value you, and I desire to be close to you in every sense of the word." Communication must fully transcend the physical to weave emotional and psychological strands into a relationship.

Examine the tale of Emma and Jack in this narrative. They are both in their late thirties and are commemorating their fifteenth anniversary of marriage. Through everything, their close relationship has been a guiding light—a beacon of optimism and reassurance that they are more than just partners but also lovers, friends, and confidants. They have faced financial difficulties and health scares together. Their love and commitment to one another have kept them from falling off the edge numerous times because of this feature of their relationship.

The message is plain to all parties involved—newlyweds, eager learners, seasoned spouses, and relationship improvers alike: undervaluing the importance of a healthy sexual life in your marriage is like disregarding the foundation of your home. Long-term stability is not guaranteed, as the very edifice you've laboriously constructed is at risk of developing cracks.

It is possible to convey love, desire, acceptance, vulnerability, and other emotions through sexual intercourse. There, we reveal our true selves, strip off the masks we wear for the outside world, and lay naked our hearts. Trust and intimacy are fundamental to every long-lasting marriage, and this degree of transparency and honesty is the cornerstone.

Additionally, this chapter clarifies the realities of preserving a solid sexual bond during a marriage. Understanding one another's wants and desires, striking a balance, and remaining receptive to inquiry and dialogue are all important. It admits that the stresses of life, whether they include work, kids, or just passing the time, can stifle desire, but that passion can be reignited with deliberate effort.

The story that runs through these pages is essentially an ode to the value of sex as a connector, a giver of happiness, and a channel of communication in a married relationship. This is a request that all couples acknowledge, value, and give attention to this area of their relationship. Tom and Sarah come to mind. They re-established their emotional and physical connection and strengthened their bond beyond measure with time, patience, and a willingness to learn about and comprehend each other's needs.

Let me conclude by saying that if you believe that "sex doesn't matter," you should reconsider. Love, connection, communication, and mutual respect are essential to a happy marriage and make an act meaningful beyond the act itself. The rewards— a deeper, more satisfying relationship—are indescribably worth the effort, knowledge, and open heart required along this voyage of discovery.

Remember to set a high bar for yourself in terms of how you express thankfulness.

It is critical to place equal, if not greater, emphasis on the "bright side," as this will assist you in developing what I refer to as "healthy emotional storage." The objective should be to have at least a three-to-one ratio of positive remarks to negative statements.

Chapter Summary

The importance of communication and physical closeness in marriage is emphasised throughout this chapter. It challenges the widespread belief that "sex doesn't matter," emphasising how important and healthy sexual closeness is for a happy marriage. The story shows how physical intimacy and open conversation about sexual preferences may greatly increase marital satisfaction and stability through examples from real-life couples like Emma and Jack and Sarah and Tom. Sex is presented as an essential manifestation of love, trust, and connection, exploring the psychological and emotional dimensions of intimacy. As the chapter comes to a close, the authors encourage couples to view their sexual relationship as the cornerstone of their marriage and promote a healthy balance between open communication about needs and desires and positive reinforcement.

Important Points

It's All About Communication: A good and fulfilling sexual relationship within a marriage depends on open and honest communication about sexual preferences and aspirations.

The Value of Close Physical Contact: Beyond merely satisfying biological requirements, physical intimacy, including sex, is a fundamental form of communication and connection between partners.

Taking Misconceptions Apart: The chapter refutes the widespread notion that having sex is not necessary for a marriage, emphasising that it is vital to the emotional and psychological health of the union.

Real-World Illustrations: The narrative illustrates the significance of physical and emotional closeness on the strength and happiness of a marriage through the accounts of couples such as Emma and Jack and Sarah and Tom.

Positive Reinforcement's Function: stressing the importance of using a positive attitude in communicating and advocating for a 3:1 ratio of encouraging remarks to critical ones to develop what is known as "healthy emotional storage."

Important Takeaways

Sex as a Form of Expression: Intimacy is a special way for partners to communicate their love, desire, acceptance, and vulnerability to each other, which builds a stronger bond and sense of trust.

The Mask of Indifference: Downplaying the significance of sex can cause a physical and emotional distance that threatens the foundation of a marriage.

Managing Life and Desire: Recognising that outside factors might stifle a person's desire for sex but stressing that couples can rekindle their passion with work and communication.

The Value of Comprehension The importance of appreciating and comprehending one another's sexual preferences and demands to have a satisfying sexual relationship.

Mutual Effort and Growth: As part of their broader commitment to one another and their marriage, the chapter emphasises the importance of both partners actively engaging in fostering their sexual relationship.

Practical Exercises

Desire notebook: For a week, each partner records in their notebook the times and situations in which they had sexual desire. Share and discuss your discoveries to improve your understanding of each other's patterns.

Communication Practice: Schedule time each week to have candid conversations about your sexual connection, with an emphasis on constructively expressing your wants and wishes.

The Positive Reinforcement Challenge is to consciously say three good things to your partner for every negative one for a month, observing any changes in the dynamics of the relationship.

Establish a monthly "intimacy date night" where the two of you explore each other's sexual impulses without the pressure of having sex. This is a great way to strengthen your emotional and physical bond.

Establish a secure area where you may talk about any insecurities or vulnerabilities you may have regarding your sexual connection. Talk about ways you may help each other while carefully listening without passing judgment.

Reflection Time

How can I tell my spouse about my sexual wants and desires right now, and how can I make this communication better?

_____
_____
_____
_____
_____
_____
_____
_____
_____
_____
_____
_____

Samantha Nunez Chapman

What are the possible ways that my fear of rejection or vulnerability is preventing me from expressing my physical affection or sexual desires?

How do the stresses of everyday life impact my sexual relationship, and how can we work together to lessen these effects?

Samantha Nunez Chapman

How can I improve our emotional storage and foster a more fulfilling sexual relationship with my spouse by consistently expressing positive affirmations to them?

After considering the tales of Sarah and Tom and Emma and Jack, what insights can I draw for my marriage to help cultivate a more fulfilling and intimate relationship?

Samantha Nunez Chapman

CHAPTER TEN

It All Starts With Cultivating A Positive Relationship With Oneself

TO BE A BETTER WIFE, YOU DON'T HAVE TO MAKE MORE MONEY or change too much at once.
Instead, start to build a loving, healthy relationship with yourself instead of being mean to yourself. The more female friends you have outside of your marriage, the more likely it is that you will get feminine support when things are going bad in your life.

It's also important for your health and happiness as a wife for you to have a self-care practice, as well as a routine for restoring your mind, body, and spirit.
Take part in a group exercise class or sign up for a yoga class every week, so that when you return to your marriage, you'll be ready to play, be curious, and support your partner as they need.

Finally, make sure that you get enough nutrition and healthy food every day to keep your energy levels stable. If you don't eat, your partner will think you're emotionally absent and emotionally unstable because you don't have any brain power.

To be happy and energetic around your partner, you need to make sure that you're taking care of your body.
Two people in a good marriage want to show their partner that they love and respect them in concrete, tangible ways that say "I love you" and "I respect you."

The best couples try to show how much they love and respect each other. You should be thinking about ways to make your spouse feel this love and respect.

Find out what you can do to make your spouse think they are important and loved. What do you do or say that makes your spouse feel disrespected? Find out what you do or say that makes them feel that way, and change it.

"The 8 Most Powerful Love Languages" might help you figure out how you and your partner naturally give and receive love as a pair. Then, talk to each other in that language, too.

Always treat your husband with respect.

For women who want to be better wives and improve their marriages, my number one advice is to always be respectful of their husbands.

Respect for your husband will inevitably affect the other areas of your marriage if you don't have respect for him.

Wives criticizing and speaking disrespectfully about their husbands in public is something I hear all the time. Sometime when the husband is present, and other times when he is not in the room.

They may do this because they are frustrated with specific behaviors or habits that their husband exhibits, or they may do it because they are speaking out of their own set of anxieties. Finally, the wife comes across as being unattractive throughout the film.

Also, I'm willing to bet that if women are speaking so negatively about their husbands in public, that they are also speaking negatively about their husbands in private.

It is unacceptable for one spouse to be rude to the other, regardless of when, why, or where it occurs. You are undermining your husband and your relationship as a result of your actions.

Kelvin and I do not always see things the same way. We all become irritated with one another from time to time. We may not always agree with one other, but we

always love and respect one another. We are always considerate of one another's feelings. Conflicts are settled on a regular basis and we move on. Despairing and damaging statements damage and harm our partnership.
As a result, whether we are in the quiet of our own homes or out in public with family or friends, we always treat one another with kind and consideration.

There are peaks of delight and troughs of hardship amidst the varied and lovely topography of a marriage journey. The idea that improving a marriage starts with the individual rather than with two people is fundamental to navigating this terrain successfully. The foundation of our investigation in Chapter Eight is this truth: "It all starts with cultivating a positive relationship with oneself."

Think about it, if you will, the tale of Anna, a devoted wife, and mother of two, whose marriage had once been characterized by mutual support and laughter but had now devolved into a series of discussions and quiet dinners, and the pivotal moment occurred on a soggy Tuesday night when, in an uncommon calm period, Anna discovered an old journal from her time in college. She was struck by her younger self's dreams and lively energy as she turned the pages. It served as a moving reminder of a side of herself that had gradually faded over the years as she put other people's needs before her own. Anna's journey to reclaiming her value and, ultimately, reviving her marriage began with this self-reflection moment.

The story of Anna highlights an important idea: a person's relationship with oneself is the cornerstone of a strong, sustaining marriage. Although everyone acknowledges this, the numerous responsibilities and obligations people take on in life can cast a shadow over it. But maintaining this inner garden is neither a luxury nor a self-serving endeavor—instead, it's a necessary habit that benefits one's connections and oneself.

To begin this technique, one must first become self-aware. This is the conscious process of looking inward to recognise and comprehend one's needs, wants, and thoughts. It's about realising your inner world's vastness, boundaries, and ideals. Take the example of Thomas, an engineer, who, through self-examination, discovered that his persistent irritation was a sign of his unfulfilled need for artistic expression rather than his partner's behavior. This insight caused him to radically change how he approached his relationship, turning disagreement into a conversation about what he needed to feel supported.

Self-awareness leads to self-compassion, the gentle acceptance of one's shortcomings and imperfections as part of one's identity. Imagine Leah, whose quick temper caused her to blame herself for marital conflict. By learning to be self-compassionate, Leah could forgive herself for her flaws and accept that they did not define who she was or her ability to love and be loved. This self-compassion became the cornerstone for constructing resilience against the unavoidable difficulties of married life.

Furthermore, developing a healthy relationship with oneself is a lifelong process. It entails establishing objectives for oneself, partaking in joyful and fulfilling pursuits, and never stopping to learn and grow. For example, Michael discovered that making time each week to follow his painting interests enhanced his sense of self and restored vitality and creativity in his relationships with his partner.

Developing a healthy relationship with oneself in marriage cannot be emphasised. It is the source of the resilience, empathy, and strength required for a successful partnership. It's about striving, learning, and being self-aware while being a whole person—not flawless. This interior balance radiates outward, bringing to the marriage tones of comprehension, endurance, and profound, lasting love.

Chapter Summary

The simple yet deep notion that changing oneself, rather than the other person or the dynamics between the two, is the first step towards improving one's marriage. In order to be a better partner, it emphasises how important it is to have a healthy connection with oneself. It emphasises the value of self-care, respect, communication, and understanding amongst people through captivating stories and useful suggestions. The chapter provides real-world examples to show how people may ensure they bring their best selves into a marriage by taking care of their personal needs before transforming their marital connections. It places a strong emphasis on the value of self-awareness, self-compassion, and ongoing personal development, providing a stable framework for a devoted, respectful, and long-lasting marriage.

Important Points

Cultivating a constructive self-relationship emphasises the importance of self-love and self-care as requirements for making a constructive contribution to a marriage.

The importance of female friendships and support is covered, along with how having outside friendship support helps stabilise emotions and strengthen a marriage.

Practices of Self-Care: This section emphasises the need to sustain mental and physical health through self-care practices, exercise, and proper diet.

Respect and Communication: Promotes the idea of respectful communication, the identification of one's love language, and the awareness of the negative consequences of receiving negative feedback from the public.

Encourages constant introspection and personal development to maintain a solid marriage in The Continuous Journey of Self-Improvement.

Important Takeaways

The Link Between Self-Love and Marital Happiness: A good self-relationship fosters positive and respectful attitudes inside a marriage, which enhances marital relationships.

The Influence of Outside Friendships and Support Systems: Outside of marriage, friendships and support systems are essential for fostering emotional fortitude and perspective.

The Significance of Physical and Emotional Self-Care: Regular self-care routines directly affect emotional stability and energy levels, which in turn affect one's involvement in the marriage.

Respect as a Fundamental Pillar: The dignity and stability of a married relationship depend heavily on respect, both in private and public.

Personal Development and Self-Awareness Fuel Marital Growth: These two factors have a major role in the dynamics of marriage, enabling deeper understanding and connection between partners.

Practical Exercises

Self-Care Routine: Make weekly time for self-care practices that revitalise your body, mind, and soul, such as yoga, meditation, or exercise.

Gratitude notebook: To cultivate a positive outlook on your relationship, keep a daily gratitude notebook in which you highlight the qualities of both you and your partner that you value.

Love Language Discovery: After taking the questionnaire with your significant other, discuss how to apply each of the "5 Love Languages" to your everyday life to learn about each other's preferred methods of showing and receiving love.

Nutrition Plan: Consider how your interactions with your partner are impacted by creating a nutritious food plan that nourishes your body to sustain energy levels and emotional equilibrium.

Respect Reflection: Consider how you and your partner have felt disrespected and respected. Talk about these instances to learn how to express respect more effectively.

Reflection Time

How does the way I see myself impact the way I see my partner?

_____
_____
_____
_____
_____
_____
_____
_____
_____
_____
_____
_____
_____
_____
_____

How can I build strong female connections to support my marriage and mental health in general?

_____
_____
_____
_____
_____
_____
_____
_____
_____
_____

Samantha Nunez Chapman

What self-care rituals have I overlooked, and what potential benefits could I reap from resuming these?

Is there a time when I haven't treated my partner with respect, especially in public? What actions can I take to ensure that I always speak with respect?

In what ways will this help my marriage, and how can I dedicate myself to a lifelong journey of self-improvement?

CHAPTER ELEVEN

Make A Conscious Effort to Date And Get to Know One Another

LISTENING WELL IS A CRITICAL SKILL FOR MAINTAINING A SUCCESSFUL MARRIAGE. This ability, which is frequently disregarded, forms the foundation of any long-lasting relationship's intricate system. Understanding your partner's feelings, intentions, and thoughts behind their words is just as important as hearing what they have to say. Becoming a better listener is a route worth taking for recently married couples, enthusiastic learners, seasoned partners, and those who are committed to strengthening their bonds.

Imagine that, following a demanding day, you are seated across from your spouse. Although they are easy to be around, every chat serves as a springboard for a closer bond. To listen genuinely is to pay attention to the underlying meanings of what is being said and the surface level of what is being spoken. Proper understanding is nurtured in the pauses, the sighs, and the vulnerable moments.

Tom and Sarah, who recently marked their fifth wedding anniversary, provide a poignant illustration of the transformational potential of listening. Early in their marriage, their conversations frequently felt like two monologues going on simultaneously, with each of them anxious to express their point of view and infrequently taking the time to consider the other truly. They didn't realize how much their relationship had changed until they consciously adjusted their strategy and put listening above replying. One evening, Sarah remembers Tom talking about his difficulties at work. Sarah gave Tom the freedom to speak without interruption by choosing to listen to him rather than making quick fixes. More honest, encouraging, and meaningful conversations between them resulted from this act of listening.

A loving act is listening, which acknowledges the importance and validity of the other person's ideas and feelings. It calls for tolerance, the ability to temporarily set aside one's ideas, and the empathy to put oneself in the other person's position. Listening well can diffuse tensions, establish mutual respect, and create an atmosphere where both parties feel heard and seen.

Think about the method of reflective listening, which involves repeating to your partner what they have said to ensure you understand them correctly. This creates room for discussion and a better understanding while demonstrating your attention to detail. Try saying something like, "What I'm hearing is..." or "It sounds like you're feeling..." in response to your partner when they share something important with you. This strategy fosters a climate of respect and understanding and validates their perspective.

Being a good listener involves accepting vulnerability in addition to practical considerations. It's about being in the moment with your spouse—both happy and uncertain—and all the moments in between. The essence of listening is recognising that every emotion has a place in the human experience and that every word you speak strengthens and beautifies your relationship.

Finally, one of the greatest gifts you can give your spouse is the act of actually listening. It shows your love, dedication, and readiness to develop a relationship. Remember that listening is the cornerstone of long-lasting love as you consciously work to date and get to know one another. Allow your partner's voice to play a special note in your life's symphony, a tune you know by heart.

Find out what your and your spouse's love languages are! Communicate with him in his love language and teach him how to communicate with you in your love language. Also, spend time together having FUN rather than just focusing on chores, cleaning, or parenting difficulties.

Next, continue conscious effort to date and get to know one another!
In the end, if there is something that bothers you, gently bring it to your partner's attention and tell him what you would prefer him to do instead of tearing apart the flaws in what he has done.

Be A Good Listener

Despite the fact that my husband and I have been together for 15 years, we have only been married for 8 years. We had our first meeting in March of 2007.
We were both very young people attempting to begin a genuine relationship, and boy did we succeed. We had already been dating for nine years when we decided to tie the knot. Ideally, we didn't expect it to have a significant impact on our relationship or responsibilities because we already felt like we were a married couple in our minds. We were completely mistaken.

The two of us developed a newfound respect for one another, and I recall feeling as if I had been given the opportunity to start again as Tallulah Nunez Chapman. Tallulah Nunez Murray, as far as I was aware, was no longer alive.
When I was younger and looking for love, I used to tell myself that I would make a wonderful wife to any man who would accept me.

Cooking, cleaning, nurturing, and being intimate with my spouse were all aspects of being a great wife to me. I had a great deal to learn.

Following our marriage, I began to sense that something was lacking on my end of the bargain. My husband was content, but I was dissatisfied with my performance as a wife. It was little, but I was able to find out what it was by listening carefully.

After a while of being together, my spouse developed into a better partner as a result of his increased attention to and observation of me. He discovered what made me tick, as well as what caused me to cry or suffer. It was simple to figure out what made me happy, but studying me in order to learn more about me transformed him into the best husband anyone could have asked for.

So it was my chance to speak. I was doing everything expected of me as a wife, with the exception of actually listening to my husband talk.

I could hear him all the time, but I wasn't really paying attention to him. He would tell me about his day, and I would only half-listen to what he was saying. It was he who would give me pointers or his viewpoint, and I would just half-heartedly follow them because I dismissed his recommendations. Then he'd tell me the stove was hot, and I'd tell him it wasn't and I'd be burned as a result.
At some point, I realized that my spouse needed me to be more present in his life. I was always physically present, but I wasn't really vocal or cooperative in the relationship, despite my physical presence. In the end, I was more concerned with myself and what I want or required.

I was content as long as he was well-fed, well-cared for, and sexually satisfied. I began to realize that he wasn't talking to me as much as he used to, or that he was talking to others who were more attentive. That's when I realized I needed to improve my listening skills.

Samantha Nunez Chapman

I put an end to my own worries and started paying attention to everything else he was saying instead of dwelling on the minutiae.
His day was told to me in the car after work. I listened to his business ideas and even gave him some advice. I took his advice into account and stopped asking other people for their advice as well or instead.
I took his parenting advice into account and stopped acting like I always knew the right thing to do. His goals, dreams, and stories made me want to do the same things.

A bigger force was formed when I started to listen. Teamwork has become a lot more real for us now. After all this time, I'm going to learn from him as well.
How he thinks and what makes him happy are things I know. I also know how he thinks and what makes him tick. We are now married, not just husband and wife.

Chapter Summary

The importance of listening in fostering and preserving a happy marriage is emphasised in this chapter. Readers are led to improve their understanding of their spouses and fortify their relationships through helpful guidance, moving anecdotes, and thoughtful thoughts. The story demonstrates listening as an expression of empathy, deference, and affection in addition to being an act of hearing. It captures the transforming ability of listening to settle disputes, promote respect for one another, and provide the groundwork for enduring love. The chapter also highlights the need to make a consistent effort to date and get to know one another, emphasising how ongoing marriage development and understanding are.

Important Points

The Cornerstone of Any Lasting Relationship is Listening: Listening emphasises knowledge beyond words to encompass gestures, pauses, and emotions.

Exemplars of Transformation: The chapter demonstrates how listening first can improve intimacy and communication in a marriage with the tale of Tom and Sarah.

Realistic Techniques: To improve communication and ensure their partners feel heard and understood, readers can benefit from an exploration of reflective listening and its practical applications.

As an Act of Love: The chapter makes the case that listening is a crucial manifestation of love that strengthens the marriage by confirming each partner's thoughts and feelings.

The Ongoing Process of Understanding The chapter emphasises the value of consistently trying to listen, learn, and develop as a pair while highlighting the author's story and marital path.

Important Takeaways

Listening Exceeds Words: Genuine listening is paying attention to not just what is stated but also to what is not uttered, including feelings, reluctance, and unsaid phrases.

Vulnerability and Presence: A good listener recognises that every word and emotion expressed is a chance to strengthen the relationship. Therefore, he or she must be both vulnerable and completely present.

Using Reflective Audience as a Tool: In addition to being a technique, reflective listening demonstrates to your partner that you value and acknowledge their views and feelings.

Constant Work Is Essential: It is important to remember that improving as a partner through listening is a continual process, emphasising the need for constant effort when dating and getting to know one another.

Marriage as a Team Effort: The chapter presents marriage as a cooperative endeavour in which both parties strengthen the union by supporting, understanding, and listening to one another.

Practical Exercises

Daily Check-Ins: Set aside time every day to talk about your feelings and actively listen without interrupting or giving uninvited advice.

Engage in a weekly conversation in which your only goal is to reflect on your partner's words, making sure you have grasped their viewpoint before answering. This is known as the reflective listening practice.

Plan a "listening date night," where you spend the evening listening to each other talk about whatever comes to mind, whether memories, anxieties, or dreams, without passing judgment or interjecting.

Empathy Walks: Go for walks with your partner and talk about important things to you, trying to understand their point of view.

Feedback Sessions: Discuss how well you feel you've been listened to and offer suggestions for improvement to each other regularly.

Reflection Time

How did you feel the last time you were genuinely listened to by your partner?

_____
_____
_____
_____
_____
_____
_____
_____
_____
_____
_____
_____
_____
_____
_____

When did you last listen intently enough to resolve a quarrel more successfully?

_____
_____
_____
_____
_____
_____
_____
_____
_____

Samantha Nunez Chapman

_____
_____
_____
_____
_____
_____

What attitudes and respect do you have for your partner are reflected in the way you listen to them?

_____
_____
_____
_____
_____
_____
_____
_____
_____
_____
_____
_____
_____
_____
_____
_____

How can you become a better listener to help you and your partner connect more deeply?

_____
_____
_____

What effects might reflective listening have on your relationship's general dynamics?

CHAPTER TWELVE

Communicate Your Needs

COUPLES ARE PRONE TO FALLING INTO THE COMFORTABILITY trap on a regular basis. Everyday life becomes normal, and self-care and romance are pushed to the sidelines. It is critical for us, as women, to take care of ourselves on a regular basis.

Get away from your husband and children for a few hours to pamper yourself. You can accomplish this by scheduling a massage session, driving around for 30 minutes alone yourself, or making it a priority to have a girls' night or weekend.

Additionally, we are apprehensive about telling our partners what we actually require and desire from them, as well as asking them what makes them happy. By articulating our wants to our partner and providing what we desire to our relationship, we are drawn closer to our spouse, rekindling the flame of love between us.

The art of communication serves as a beacon in the marriage sphere, where two hearts promise to share life's journey through calm and stormy waters. In keeping with this attitude, we explore the meaning of communicating one's wants, vital to fostering the connection that binds spirits in marital harmony. While it may appear simple, communicating your needs requires grace and resolve since it's a complex dance of vulnerability, courage, and understanding.

Say you could picture Eleanor and Michael, who have been together for two years, curled up in their small living room on a calm afternoon. The walls are softly coated in golden sunset tones, creating a cozy radiance that symbolizes their shared love. Eleanor, however, is hiding a sense of unfulfillment and an unsaid need for a deeper emotional connection beneath this picture-perfect exterior. Michael doesn't notice how alone his wife is becoming since he is too preoccupied with the chaos of his new job.

This incident reveals the crucial need to communicate one's wants, typical of the marriage tapestry. From quiet to articulation, Eleanor's story reflects the struggles and victories that many couples experience. Her ability to communicate her emotions to Michael is a sign of trust and self-expression since it gives him a glimpse into her personal life.

Self-reflection is the first step in this communicative dance. Before Eleanor could articulate her demands, she went inward, examining the shapes of her wants and the sources of her needs. This self-examination is the only way to understand what is lacking genuinely, what needs to be nurtured, and what ambitions are waiting to be pursued together.

Equipped with discernment, Eleanor selected a peaceful moment to let Michael into her heart, away from the interruptions of everyday life. Her tactful but forceful manner was an invitation rather than an indictment. She spoke in "I" statements, which are vulnerable and avoid placing blame while promoting empathy. "These days, I feel a little disengaged, and I miss our in-depth discussions. I need us to spend more time together alone so that we can establish a stronger bond."

Right now, Michael's answer could determine how their marriage develops. The act of sharing and the reaction that follows are both beautiful aspects of expressing one's needs. Michael was initially surprised, but he listened with an open heart, and his love for Eleanor helped him overcome his first defensiveness. After having this crucial talk, which served as a bridge to understanding, they decided to incorporate "us time"—time set aside each week to rekindle their emotional connection and spend time together—into their routine.

Eleanor and Michael's journey serves as an example of how communicating one's wants may have a transforming effect. It draws attention to how crucial timing, tone, and empathy are—elements that, when combined, weave a tapestry of increased closeness and comprehension. Through each whispered dream and shared experience, they learned that this procedure is a journey rather than a destination.

In a married relationship, when every day is a fresh chapter in a standard narrative, expressing one's wants to one's spouse is a sign of mutual love and self-love. It serves as a foundation for the marriage edifice, guaranteeing that the winds of change and adversity will only fortify the bonds of love.

Remember this: the honesty of your communication makes your marriage strong. This applies to newlyweds setting out on this journey, enthusiastic learners hoping to strengthen their relationship, and seasoned spouses hoping to revitalize their union. By being upfront and honest about your wants, you create a space for intimacy and understanding and a haven for true love to grow.

Chapter Summary

In "Communicate Your Needs," honest and transparent communication in a married relationship is discussed as a fundamental component for preserving and strengthening the bond. The story emphasises couples' difficulties when they give in to comfort, forget their needs and wants, and lose interest in romance and self-care. The narrative of Eleanor and Michael serves as an example for readers to understand the challenges and benefits of clearly expressing one's demands. This chapter strongly emphasises introspection, having the guts to speak one's mind, and realising how important it is to build understanding between people to keep the flame of love alive.

Important Points

The Value of Self-Care Emphasises on how important it is for people, especially women, to prioritise self-care in order to preserve their wellbeing and, consequently, improve their marriages.

Communication Challenge: It discusses the shared anxiety of expressing one's own needs and desires in a married relationship as well as the advantages of both parties knowing what makes the other happy.

Eleanor and Michael's Story: This story highlights the transforming potential of open communication by illuminating the complex dynamics of a relationship battling unspoken needs.

The significance of self-reflection in recognising one's own needs and desires prior to proficiently conveying them to a spouse is emphasised in this piece.

The Practice of Effective Communication: Provides guidance on how to have productive talks about needs, supporting the use of "I" statements and timing your words to foster understanding and empathy.

Important Takeaways

The First Step in Communication is Self-Reflection. It takes reflection to comprehend one's own wants completely. Before you start talking to your spouse, it is important to know what you both lack, want, or want to accomplish together.

For Both Partners, Empathy Is Essential: Communication and the relationship as a whole can be greatly improved by having the capacity to understand each other's thoughts and feelings.

Defensiveness hinders Connection: Building an atmosphere of openness and trust requires overcoming early defensive responses to criticism or demands communicated by a partner.

Planned "Us Time" Strengthens Connections: Maintaining the strength of the marriage depends greatly on regularly scheduled time spent discussing and rekindling emotional connections.

A solid foundation is built on honesty and integrity in communication between spouses. A marriage's strength and resiliency are largely dependent on this.

Practical Activities

Self-Treatment Programme: Establish a weekly time slot for reflective activities related to your needs and desires as a form of personal self-care.

Practice Making Clearly and Empathetically Stated "I" Statements: Make a list of the needs or sentiments you would like to share with your spouse and then frame them in "I" statements.

Role-playing Active Listening: Take turns sharing a need or worry with your partner while the other actively listens without interjecting or getting combative.

Scheduling Weekly "Us Time": Plan each week when you can be together, communicate, and spend quality time together without interruptions.

Keep a Thankfulness Diary Together where you can record your appreciation for one another and talk about it when you have some "us time."

Reflection Time

What areas of self-care do I frequently overlook that could improve my ability to recognise and express my needs?

_____
_____
_____
_____
_____
_____
_____
_____
_____
_____
_____
_____
_____
_____
_____

How can I feel more at ease being vulnerable when I share my wants and worries with my partner?

_____
_____
_____

Samantha Nunez Chapman

How can I respond less defensively to my partner's attempts to express their needs?

How imaginatively can we use "us time" to make sure we're frequently connecting more deeply?

_____
_____
_____
_____
_____
_____
_____
_____
_____
_____
_____
_____
_____
_____
_____
_____
_____

How does practising thankfulness affect our capacity to communicate and attend to one another's needs?

_____
_____
_____
_____
_____
_____
_____
_____

CHAPTER THIRTEEN

Tell Him How Good He Is In Bed

MARRIAGE IS A RELATIONSHIP IN WHICH EXPRESSING GRATITUDE TO ONE'S spouse, particularly in the private space of the bedroom, maybe both a healing and a stimulating force for a closer bond. The act of "Tell Him How Good He Is In Bed" expresses vulnerability, communication, and sincere appreciation of the pleasure you share rather than just feeding your ego. This appreciation can strengthen the bonds between you and your partner by introducing intimacy and respect into your relationship.

For a brief while, picture Sarah and Tom as a couple entangled in the routine and stillness a few years into their marriage. Their evenings were spent dancing quietly in avoidance; their days were occupied with the unsaid. Not until a weekend away, a unique time of quiet without the kids, did Sarah inhale deeply and murmur to Tom, in the shadow of the night, words of genuine gratitude. It was a statement that expressed gratitude for all of his hard work and affection in creating beautiful moments of intimacy. The impact was both profound and instantaneous. Tom's eyes brightened with pride, and he also realized that his wife had seen him. A spark that had been fading due to the stress of everyday living was rekindled by it.

An important marriage lesson shown by this incident is the need for communication, particularly regarding the positive elements of your partnership. Focusing on areas that require improvement or where friction exists is a common mistake. However, growth and intimacy are fostered by enjoying what is lovely and enjoyable.

By complimenting your spouse on his bed manners, you are fostering an honest conversation about your sexual partnership. It's an invitation for him to express his hopes and anxieties, just like you do. This vulnerability makes a more rewarding and exciting sexual life possible. It's not just about the physical act; it's also about emotional connection and being seen and valued when one is most vulnerable.

Additionally, there may be repercussions for other aspects of your marriage from this verbal appreciation exercise. It strengthens the positive and appreciative culture in your relationship, simplifying overcoming obstacles together. You foster an atmosphere conducive to love when you emphasize the good things in life and make it a habit to express what brings you joy and fulfillment.

Still, it's important to remember that authenticity counts. The goal here is to express sincere gratitude for the intimacy, and connection shared not just lip service. Acknowledging your partner's efforts to create enjoyable and satisfying sexual experiences is also essential.

Telling your spouse how wonderful he is in bed shows love and respect. It recognizes the work, openness, and closeness of being close. Amid life's chaos, it serves as a reminder that you see each other, value each other, and are dedicated to fostering happiness and enjoyment together.

The narrative of Sarah and Tom illustrates the potency of these acknowledgement moments. It reminds us that expressions of gratitude may be a significant gift inside the sacred space of marriage, strengthening bonds, increasing intimacy, and honing the love that brought us together.

Samantha Nunez Chapman

Chapter Summary

"Tell Him How Good He IS In Bed" explores the powerful effects that showing gratitude to a partner, particularly in the private space of the bedroom, may have on preserving a marriage. Couples can strengthen their bond and bring intimacy and respect into their relationship by being vulnerable, communicating, and showing genuine appreciation for one another. The story of Sarah and Tom shows a heartwarming illustration of how a spouse's efforts to create meaningful moments of intimacy can reignite a marriage. This gesture of gratitude not only strengthens the bond between partners sexually but also improves the relationship dynamic by promoting respect, love, and progress for both parties.

Important Points

Expressing Gratitude: Expressing gratitude in marriage, especially during private moments, is crucial for promoting a closer bond and respect between partners.

Vulnerability and Communication: Talking freely and honestly about one's sexual relationship can make it easier to have a fulfilling and interesting sexual life.

Positive Reinforcement is the process of highlighting and valuing the good parts of a partnership to foster development and closeness.

Emotional Connection: The importance of feeling recognised and appreciated at one's most vulnerable times.

Genuine Appreciation: Sincerity is essential when expressing thanks to ensure it is received seriously and builds the relationship.

Important Takeaways

Beyond Physical Contact: True intimacy goes beyond physical contact to include emotional ties and shared vulnerability.

Recognising Your Strengths: Relationships can undergo a metamorphosis when passion and intimacy are rekindled by acknowledging and appreciating another person's efforts.

Positive Feedback Loop: When behaviours and acts that fortify a partner's bond are reinforced and appreciated, they can generate a feedback loop that encourages more of the same.

Building a Culture of Thankfulness: Regular acts of thankfulness help create a relationship culture that values optimism and appreciation for one another.

Getting Over Obstacles Together: Partners who have a solid foundation of appreciation and respect for one another may find it simpler to confront and overcome challenges.

Practical Exercises

Gratitude notebook: Each spouse maintains a private notebook for one week to record moments of thankfulness for their partnership, particularly in the bedroom. At the end of the week, exchange these entries with one another.

Create an Appreciation Ritual: Tell your partner something you value about them every day or week, such as their attempts to keep the relationship intimate.

Vulnerability Exercise: To strengthen your emotional bond, have an honest conversation about your aspirations, anxieties, and desires for your sexual relationship.

Positive Reinforcement: Remember to compliment your partner on something particular that you both loved about your private time together.

Consider a recent intimate occasion and express gratitude for your partner's efforts and your shared vulnerability. Then, in a sincere discussion, discuss your ideas.

Reflection Time

How can I get better at thanking my partner for their accomplishments in our personal life? What are some of the ways I presently do this?

_____
_____
_____
_____
_____
_____
_____
_____
_____
_____
_____
_____
_____
_____

How at ease am I talking to my partner about our sexual connection in an honest and vulnerable way, and what actions can we take to improve our communication?

_____
_____
_____
_____
_____
_____
_____
_____
_____

Think back to when your significant other showed you gratitude for your work. What was your reaction to it, and why?

How might cultivating an attitude of thankfulness in our partnership help us get through the difficulties we face together?

Samantha Nunez Chapman

How can I express my thankfulness in a more genuine way and true to our closeness and profound connection?

CHAPTER FOURTEEN

Aid His Friendships

UNDERSTANDING AND SUPPORTING YOUR PARTNER'S TREASURED friendships can be the foundation of a robust and happy marriage. It goes beyond just putting up with his social events and listening obligingly to him talk about his pals. It's important to actively support these connections since you understand how much they affect his well-being and, consequently, the strength of your marriage.

Think about Emma and Liam's story. After five years of marriage, Emma realized Liam frequently talked about his college days with people he no longer saw. Emma experienced a brief jealousy attack. When he had her, why did Liam need these old contacts? But when she heard more, she saw that these friendships were essential to Liam's identity and had nothing to do with excluding her.

Emma decided to take action. She planned a surprise get-together for Liam and his college pals. It was impossible to miss the happiness in Liam's eyes upon seeing his old buddies. That night, Emma saw more in Liam than simply the impressionable, carefree boy from the media; she saw a side of her husband that deepened their bond.

This narrative emphasizes how important it is to support your husband's friendships. It has to do with accepting his universe outside of your joint existence. By doing this, you enhance rather than lessen the significance of your relationship. **Here's how you can proactively encourage his friendships:**

Promote Independence: Persuade him to get out with his pals alone. A married couple should have their own hobbies and social networks. Because each spouse brings fresh insights and experiences to their shared existence, this independence can result in a more satisfying partnership.

Express Sincere Interest: Show concern for his pals. Inquire about their lives, remember their names, and express your partner's gratitude for them. Becoming best friends with them is unnecessary, but it will mean a lot to him to know that you are concerned about his relationships.

Organise Social Events: You may help your spouse contact his friends like Emma did. He may easily keep up these crucial relationships by throwing a dinner party or other informal get-together without worrying about the details.

Respect Boundaries: Recognise that he and his pals have private talks and sometimes engage in private activities. Respecting these limits demonstrates confidence in and regard for his autonomous connections rather than implying exclusion.

Support Through Shifts: Friendships change and sometimes become less potent. Offer your spouse your full support during these transitions. Please support and pay attention to his sentiments whenever a friendship breaks or evolves. Recall that what matters is the quality rather than the quantity of friendships.

Supporting your husband's friendships helps him be happy, which helps your marriage stay strong. It's evidence of your awareness of his identity outside his partner's role. Interacting with this more expansive area of his life enhances his experience and infuses your relationship with new vitality.

Narratives such as the one involving Emma and Liam demonstrate the significant influence of fostering these external relationships. Their story is a reminder that in a healthy marriage, both partners should expand their worlds together instead of limiting one another.

Chapter Summary

To maintain a strong and happy marriage, "Aid His Friendships" emphasises how important it is to encourage your partner's friendships. It explores the importance of appreciating these external interactions, not just putting up with them. It demonstrates, via Emma and Liam's story, how supporting your partner's friendships may strengthen the marriage, increase individual autonomy, and improve both couples' general well-being. Practical tips on encouraging independence, demonstrating sincere interest, planning social gatherings, upholding limits, and offering support through friendship transitions are included in this chapter.

Important Points

Understanding and Assistance: Acknowledging the value of your spouse's friendships and providing them with active support can improve your marriage.

Encourage Independence: Having a partner with different interests and social networks brings a variety of perspectives and experiences to the marriage.

Show Genuine Interest: Being interested in your partner's friends' lives and relationships demonstrates your respect for and appreciation of those ties.

Plan Social Events: By providing occasions for your partner to interact with his friends without adding to the stress of preparation, you may help your partner retain these vital relationships.

Recognise your boundaries: Respecting these limits and realising that certain parts of your partner's friendship are private will help to build trust and respect in your partnership.

Important Takeaways

Identity and Friendships: A partner's friendships, which are essential to their identity and general well-being, impact the health and happiness of a marriage.

Mutual Development: Encouraging one another's outside interactions fosters personal development and infuses the marriage with new ideas.

Confidence in Autonomy: You can show your partner that you have faith in their partnership by supporting their independence and honouring their private social contacts.

Change and Support: Emotional support is essential for your partner, even if it means enduring a friendship's inevitable breakdown.

Strengthened Bond: Fostering your partner's friendships honours their uniqueness and strengthens your bond with them.

Practical Exercises

Friendship Appreciation Night: Set aside a night once a month to celebrate your friendships by sharing recollections and anecdotes about each other and highlighting their significance in your life.

Interest Inventory: Enumerate your partner's close pals and make a note of anything unique about them so you may discuss it with your partner.

Organiser of Events: Make the effort to plan a lighthearted gathering for your significant other and their pals, ensuring it fits with their hobbies.

Boundaries Talk: Having an honest conversation about friendship limits makes both parties feel valued and at ease.

Samantha Nunez Chapman

Support System: Make a strategy for how, in addition to listening and providing comfort, you may be a supporting partner when your spouse's friendships shift.

Reflection Time

How do I feel about my partner's friendships now, and how can I help these connections more effectively?

_____
_____
_____
_____
_____
_____
_____
_____
_____
_____
_____
_____
_____
_____
_____

How have I shown that I genuinely care about the friends and well-being of my partner?

_____
_____
_____
_____
_____
_____

Samantha Nunez Chapman

_____
_____
_____
_____
_____
_____
_____
_____
_____

How do I support my partner's freedom without jeopardising our solid and enduring relationship?

_____
_____
_____
_____
_____
_____
_____
_____
_____
_____
_____
_____
_____
_____

Considering Emma and Liam's tale, how can I strengthen my marriage and encourage my partner's friendships?

Samantha Nunez Chapman

Samantha Nunez Chapman

CHAPTER FIFTEEN

Let Go of Your Phone

IN THE AGE OF DIGITAL WONDERS, WHEN OUR LIVES ARE ENTIRELY entangled in the light of screens, "Letting Go Of Your Phone" stands out as a ray of hope for couples facing challenges and marital joy. This idea, although it may appear straightforward, significantly impacts the structure of our close relationships.

See yourself on a calm evening. After a long day, two hearts try to reunite in the living room as the sun sets. It is a peaceful dusk. But a smartphone's incessant ping, shine, and buzz has unexpectedly joined this small party. This situation, repeated in innumerable households worldwide, gradually undermines the communication and connection bonds underpinning marriages.

Setting your phone down is more than just a practical gesture—it represents your respect, presence, and full attention for your partner. Giving your partner your entire attention in a world where it's highly valued is a sign of your dedication and affection.

Take Rachel and John's story, for example. Like many other couples, they became entangled in the web of digital distraction. Dinners were quiet events, except for the occasional screen tap. Talks broke up frequently due to the enticing nature of a notification. Their estrangement became apparent when they took a digital detox weekend. Released from the shackles of their digital devices, they rediscover the art of meaningful dialogue, the delight of belly laughs, and the reassuring stillness that speaks volumes. Their narrative serves as evidence of the transformational potential of presence.

Start modestly when you embark on this path of digital disentanglement. Set up specific times and places in your house and calendar for no electronics. Start with dinnertime and make it a sacred time to rekindle relationships away from the allure of social media and emails. By resisting the digital invasion with a modest act of disobedience, you can build stronger relationships and learn actually to listen and be heard.

Furthermore, it's critical to spend time together doing things that strengthen your relationship without technology. Whether it's a shared activity, a stroll in the embrace of nature, or just spending time together in silence while taking everything around you, these are the raw, authentic moments that form the foundation of a strong marriage.

However, the process of letting go is challenging. It's common for withdrawal symptoms from the digital world to take the form of a persistent feeling of missing something or a constant need to check one's phone. While acknowledging these emotions, keep in mind the fuller, livelier world waiting for you outside the screen. In this world, sincere connection and unwavering care are the cornerstones of a successful marriage.

"Letting Go Of Your Phone" is an invitation to reevaluate technology's place in your life and marriage, not a request to give it up completely. It's about striking a balance so that the richness and caliber of your interactions are enhanced rather than diminished by technology.

Talk Him Up

It is necessary to speak well of your husband, especially when they're not around. This idea, frequently summed up by the expression "Talk Him Up," is not just about getting compliments from others; it is the basis of mutual respect, trust, and adoration in a partnership. This practice can significantly impact the dynamics of a partnership for newlyweds, eager learners, seasoned spouses, and individuals dedicated to enhancing their relationships.

Imagine that you are attending a social event without your spouse. The subject turns to personal life, and you take advantage of the chance to talk about things other than your partner's humiliating but funny anecdotes or whine about little irritations. Instead, you take a different approach and talk him up. You acknowledge his talents, celebrate his accomplishments no matter how small, and show pride in his hard work and achievements. Despite being introductory, this action has a strong impact.

Let's explore the benefits of "Talking Him Up" and how to incorporate it tastefully into your everyday routine. First and foremost, it's critical to understand that this practice isn't about creating a façade of perfection or evading real issues that require attention. It's about focusing on the good things in life, praising your partner's attributes, and highlighting the advantages of your partnership both in public and private.

Creating an Environment of Mutual Admiration and Respect

When you speak well of your spouse, you create a culture of respect and admiration for each other. This significantly impacts how people view your relationship overall, not just how they view your partner. It expresses your dedication and confidence in your partner's value. In addition, your spouse's self-esteem is bolstered, and your relationship is strengthened when they learn of your admiration for them from others.

Real Life Story

Examine the tale of Jane and Kenneth, a married couple of five years. Even when Liam was disheartened by his lack of artistic advancement, Jane would not hesitate to compliment him on his commitment to his family and artistic endeavors. Jane's constant encouragement elevated Kenneth's spirits throughout difficult times and inspired him to keep going, resulting in him exhibiting his artwork in a nearby gallery. The help wasn't in vain; Liam felt greatly loved and appreciated, strengthening their bond and affection.

Helpful Suggestions for Including "Talk Him Up" in Your Marriage

Start Small and Be Sincere: Commence by praising your partner for the little things in life, such as their ability to calm you down when stressed or make time for family dinners. Genuineness is essential; allow your compliments to express how you genuinely feel accurately.

Please share with a Purpose: Tell friends and relatives about your spouse's accomplishments and tales that showcase their moral fiber and contributions. This is about honestly highlighting your partner's good qualities, not boasting.

Celebrate achievement Together: When your significant other achieves it, acknowledge it as a joint triumph. This demonstrates your appreciation for their objectives and pride in their achievements.

Encouragement in Times of Doubt: When your partner is going through difficult times, remind him or her of their past successes and strengths. Your self-assurance in them can work as a strong incentive.

Think and Give Thanks in Private: Tell your lover how much you appreciate them. Tell them why you think well of them and how they have improved your life.

"Talking Him Up" is a testimonial to the depth of your collaboration in the marriage experience. It's a discipline that builds an atmosphere of support, encouragement, and unconditional love within your partnership and creates a favorable outward perception. As newlyweds, long-married couples, or anybody committed to preserving their marriage, remember that the things you say and do to demonstrate your love for your spouse can have just as much of an impact as the words you use to describe them. You improve your relationship and leave a lasting legacy of respect and admiration by improving them.

Chapter Summary

"Letting Go Of Your Phone" becomes essential for strengthening bonds in marriages in a world where digital distractions are taking over. This chapter explores the widespread problem of cell phones interfering with our private time and emphasises how digital detoxification may be life-changing for couples like Rachel and John. Couples can re-discover the skill of meaningful discussion, shared laughter, and the subtle yet deep language of friendship by designating specific times and areas free from electronic gadgets. The path to digital disentanglement is portrayed as a call for balance, ensuring that our devices enhance our interactions rather than diminish them, rather than as a rejection of technology.

Important Points

Digital Distraction Weakens the Bonds of Marriage: Our phones' incessant pings and notifications prevent us from giving our spouses our attention, eroding our relationships' cornerstones.

Being present has the transformative capacity to build stronger emotional bonds with our partners. It is a great way to show our love and respect for them.

Relationship Revival Is Possible With Digital Detox: Reconnecting for a short while can enhance communication and help couples rediscover the pleasure of each other's company.

How to Disengage in Realistic Steps: Setting up electronic-free periods and areas in the house promotes face-to-face communication and mutual attention.

The objective is to strike a healthy equilibrium where technology improves rather than diminishes the calibre of married life.

Important Takeaways

Time that is not disrupted is valuable: A unique and priceless gift in this day of perpetual connectedness is setting aside time just for your mate.

Digital Routines Influence Relationship Structure: Interpersonal interactions might be unintentionally influenced by our behaviour when using our technology.

Creating a more attentive and present-oriented partnership begins with acknowledging the negative effects of digital distractions. Awareness breeds change.

Shared activities strengthen bonding: Couples' emotional relationships are strengthened when they participate in activities without using technology.

Communication Has Many Facets: Laughter, silence, and just being together in the present are all important aspects of true connection that go beyond words.

Practical Exercises

Digital Reset Date Night: Set up a regular evening for your relationship on which you will not use any electronic gadgets and will spend time together instead. Establish "tech-free zones" in your home, such as the dining room or bedroom, to encourage uninterrupted communication and interaction.

Shared Hobby Time: Decide on a pastime or pastime that both couples will like, and commit to spend time on it frequently, away from electronics.

Lists of gratitude: To strengthen the importance of your connection outside of the digital sphere, list the times or traits you respect most in each other that aren't connected to technology.

Establishing Daily Rituals for Communication: Set aside time each day, without the use of phones or other electronics, to communicate your thoughts, feelings, and experiences of the day.

Reflection Time

What effects has the availability of smartphones and other digital gadgets had on your capacity to establish a deeper connection with your partner?

_____
_____
_____
_____
_____
_____
_____
_____
_____
_____
_____
_____
_____
_____
_____
_____

Can you think of an instance when you lost a chance to connect with your partner because of a digital distraction? How did you feel about it?

_____
_____
_____

Samantha Nunez Chapman

What doable actions can you and your spouse take to spend more time together without using technology? How might these modifications strengthen your bond?

Consider how technology is used in your relationship. Are there any places where its effects are more detrimental than beneficial? How can these areas be addressed?

Samantha Nunez Chapman

How can you and your significant other help each other be more mindful and in the moment, both together and apart?

CHAPTER SIXTEEN

Give Him Some Space

REALIZING HOW IMPORTANT IT IS TO GIVE YOUR HUSBAND SPACE is similar to caring for a garden. In a marriage, both spouses need the space to develop as individuals, much as plants need room to spread their roots. Despite its apparent simplicity, this idea has essential ramifications for building a solid and close-knit relationship.

In the marriage atmosphere, especially for recentlyweds and those committed to reviving their relationship, practicing personal space tolerance might occasionally seem paradoxical. Ultimately, the blissful combination of matrimony frequently evokes visions of unceasing company and communal pursuits. However, in the delicate practice of taking a step back, we discover our connections are subtly getting more muscular, giving each partner the breathing room they need to thrive and improving the relationship's overall soil.

Think about the tale of Juliet and Tom, a couple who entered into marriage with all the zeal and affection one could desire. From early coffees in the morning to strolls in the evening, they shared every moment in the beginning. Nevertheless, as the months passed, Tom became increasingly restless. He was an ardent painter, and he had not touched his brushes since the wedding. Even if they were fun, the company had subtly replaced the quiet time he needed to work on his paintings.

Emily came across the idea of creating distance in a marriage in a casual talk with a friend. She found resonance in the idea, which led to a contemplative analysis of how to strike a balance between unity and uniqueness. She discussed the topic with

Tom that night over dinner, saying she hoped they would pursue their own interests in addition to their shared ones.

Their relationship felt different when they deliberately created time for "me time," even though the transition didn't happen immediately. Tom took up painting again and would frequently spend Sunday mornings creating paintings. For her part, Emily renewed her interest in books by joining a neighborhood book group. Beyond reviving their interests, these solitary pursuits invigorated their shared existence with new vitality and anecdotes, adding even greater significance to their time spent together.

This story emphasizes a crucial lesson: allowing space for each partner to realize their potential rather than putting them at odds with one another means giving space. A delicate balance calls for trust, understanding, and communication.

As you approach this trip, consider making time to talk about each other's privacy requirements. These could be time spent with friends, a peaceful evening of introspection, or a pastime one aspires to pursue. Recognize that these demands enhance rather than lessen your love and commitment for one another.

Recall that a marriage depends not only on the time spent together but also on personal development outside of it. By accepting the idea of space, you can create a relationship characterized by mutual respect, understanding, and a growing connection.

To sum up, allowing yourself space shows how strong your relationship is. It's a declaration that you cherish and honor each other's uniqueness and shared togetherness. Allow the principle of space to guide you as you manage the challenges of marriage, and watch as your love blossoms with resilience and brightness.

Chapter Summary

"Give Him Some Space" explains the critical role that personal space plays in marriage by drawing a comparison between it and the maintenance needed for a healthy garden. It refutes the widely held belief that marriage equals unceasing companionship and emphasises the importance of personal development and goals as the cornerstones of a solid, close partnership. Readers are taught how adding personal space into a marriage may revitalise individual interests and enhance the union through the story of Juliet and Tom. According to this section, honouring one another's need for space doesn't worsen a relationship; on the contrary, it strengthens and fosters love, respect, and understanding.

Important Points

Personal Space Is Essential for Growth: People need space in a marriage to grow and thrive, just as plants need space to spread their roots.

Strike a Healthy Balance Between Togetherness and Individuality: A happy marriage depends on striking a good balance between shared interests and personal goals.

Improved Relationship Through Personal Interests: Following one's hobbies can give a relationship new life by fostering understanding and stimulating dialogue.

To allow personal space in a marriage, you and your spouse must have mutual trust, understanding, and open communication about their needs.

Mutual Respect for Personal Growth: Acknowledging and assisting one another's needs for personal growth strengthens and deepens the marriage.

Important Takeaways

Space is Not Separation: Rather than fostering estrangement, giving someone space is about supporting their personal development and fulfilment, which enhances their marriage.

Personal Goals and Contentment Affect Marital Contentment: Personal goals and contentment are not only advantageous but also essential for a strong, happy marriage.

Clear Communication Is Essential: A closer bond and greater understanding are fostered when people discuss and accept one another's need for space.

Honouring Individuality Promotes Cohesion: The common life is enhanced when people recognise and support one another's distinctive hobbies and personalities.

The dynamic nature of married relationships necessitates flexibility and adaptability in balancing unity and individualism.

Practical Exercises

Weekly Check-in: Arrange a meeting once a week to discuss your need for alone time and group activities.

Adopt a Solo Pastime: Each couple chooses a previously unexplored or abandoned pastime to work on independently, communicating with the other about their progress and experiences.

Establish Personal Spaces: Set aside specific locations in your house for each person to use for hobbies, reading, or meditation when they have time.

Arrange Personal Travels: Encourage each other to go out alone or with friends to remind each other of the value of social interactions with people outside the home.

Think and Discuss: After some alone time to consider your aspirations, gather together to discuss how you might help one another.

Reflective Time

How do I now view personal space in my marriage, and how can I change my viewpoint to appreciate it?

_____
_____
_____
_____
_____
_____
_____
_____
_____
_____
_____
_____

What hobbies or personal interests have I ignored since marriage, and how can I start reintroducing them?

_____
_____
_____

Samantha Nunez Chapman

How can I help my partner pursue their interests and development?

How can we effectively express our need for separation without making our partnership seem bad or careless?

Thinking back on the harmony between our uniqueness and unity, what actions can we take to strengthen this harmony in our marriage?

CHAPTER SEVENTEEN

Help Him Achieve His Goals

SUPPORTING YOUR SPOUSE IN REACHING THEIR OBJECTIVES is like taking care of the core of your trip together—a journey that is both individual and group. This gesture of support is about strengthening the foundation of your marriage, not only about achieving individual goals. When you actively support your spouse's goals, you weave strands of respect, admiration, and, most crucially, partnership into the fabric of your relationship.

Take the example of Emily and Tom, a married couple of five years. Tom had always wanted to publish a novel and was a dedicated but failing writer. Alison set out to assist Tom in realizing his ambition since she saw his talent and potential. She started by designing quiet times for Tom to write at home as she knew he needed a calm atmosphere to inspire him. She also assumed more duties around the house to provide him with the required time. In addition, Alison set up Tom's attendance at a writer's workshop since she thought outside criticism was essential to Tom's development. Their accomplishment was celebrated as much as his own when Tom's book was eventually released. Their tale is a powerful example of the positive effects of encouraging your partner to pursue their dreams in a marriage.

Talk honestly and openly with your spouse about their goals before attempting to assist them in reaching them. This conversation is essential because it establishes the foundation for empathy and understanding. Respecting your partner's dreams and individuality means paying close attention to what they want from life without passing judgment or offering unsolicited advice. It's critical to remember that this is about them and their goals; your job is to be their unwavering supporter.

After you fully grasp their objectives, think of practical ways you might assist them. If your partner wants to return to school, you should offer them extra responsibilities at home so they can devote more time to their studies. Alternatively, it can entail being understanding of the late nights or extra hours they must put in if they want to progress in their work. Financial sacrifices, such as saving for an investment or a course your spouse wants to take, may also be necessary to support them.

To do this, it is essential to remain in balance. When assisting your spouse, make sure that your wants and objectives are addressed. Mutual support is essential to a happy marriage, where both spouses feel appreciated and free to follow their aspirations.

Furthermore, it's critical to commemorate each accomplishment, no matter how tiny. Celebrating and recognizing one another's accomplishments strengthens the resolve to support one another in realizing their aspirations. Taking the time to rejoice together, no matter how big or small the win, keeps your relationship strong and solidifies your connection.

In summary, supporting your partner in their endeavors is a beautiful way to show your love and dedication. It calls for tolerance, comprehension, and occasionally selflessness. But the benefits are priceless. It helps your partner feel fulfilled personally, strengthens your bond, and makes it more significant. Always remember that when one partner succeeds, the couple wins together. By fostering an environment of mutual respect, celebration, and support, you may create a long-lasting marriage based on both parties' success and happiness.

Chapter Summary

"Help Him Achieve His Goals" highlights the critical role that support plays in a marriage, stressing that assisting your partner in realising their goals is essential to fostering a solid, cohesive bond. The chapter uses Emily and Tom's story to show how supportive, understanding and helpful behaviours may greatly impact a partner's achievement and, consequently, the marriage's well-being. It provides a structure for candid communication, proactive support, preserving equilibrium, and jointly acknowledging accomplishments, all to cultivate a partnership in which both parties feel appreciated, encouraged, and inspired to achieve their goals.

Important Points

Help as the Foundation of a Partnership: By incorporating respect, appreciation, and cooperation into your spouse's goals, you may fortify the foundation of your marriage.

Open Communication: Establishing empathy and understanding is essential for laying the foundation for effective assistance. To do this, it is important to have frank and open discussions about goals.

Practical Assistance: It's crucial to comprehend your partner's requirements and provide real support, whether by making financial sacrifices, taking on more household duties, or providing possibilities for professional growth.

Balance and Mutual Support: It's critical to emphasise the value of mutual support in a relationship while supporting your spouse and ensuring that your wants and goals are not neglected.

Honouring Success: Recognising and applauding each accomplishment, no matter how minor, strengthens the relationship and shows mutual support for each other's success.

Practical Exercises

Understanding and Empathy Are Fundamental. Effective support starts with your capacity to listen to and understand your partner's dreams without passing judgment.

Encourage Transcends Material Assistance More often than not, and money gifts are surpassed by emotional support and belief in your partner's potential, which breeds motivation and self-assurance.

The Support Ripple Effect: Supporting your partner's goals can result in increased self-worth, a stronger sense of personal fulfilment, and a closer marriage between partners.

Success Is a Shared Journey: In a marriage, the accomplishment of one spouse represents a win for the other, demonstrating the interdependence of their goals and objectives.

For Longevity, a balanced partnership is essential. Ensuring that each partner feels appreciated and encouraged is essential to a successful and long-lasting marriage.

Reflection Time

To what extent do I comprehend my partner's present desires and ambitions? Have we had a thorough and honest discussion about these?

_____
_____
_____
_____
_____
_____

How have I helped my partner achieve their dreams in real life? Exist any areas where I could do better?

How do we commemorate our victories, and how does this strengthen our relationship?

Samantha Nunez Chapman

When I think back on our relationship, do we still have a good balance between our mutual support? What can we do to improve this equilibrium?

Taking into account Emily and Tom's tale, how might we use comparable tactics to encourage one another's objectives and improve our marriage?

Samantha Nunez Chapman

CHAPTER EIGHTEEN

Help Him Achieve His Goals

ONE OF THE MOST IMPORTANT THINGS YOU CAN DO FOR YOUR SPOUSE while you walk the married path is to encourage him to pursue his personal and professional aspirations. This path, sometimes disregarded, is essential to living a healthy lifestyle that promotes relationship development, fulfillment, and a sense of accomplishment.

Consider John, a painter devoted to his work but whose corporate career saps his inspiration. Sandra, his spouse, observed his waning enthusiasm and recalled his desire to organize an art show. Sandra recognized the significance of John's goals and set out to convert their garage into a temporary recording studio. She even set up a local gallery to encourage John to devote attention to his painting every weekend. John's final exhibition was more than simply an artistic display; it was evidence of a wife's faith in her husband's aspirations. This tale shows how encouraging your partner's ambitions may go beyond simple friendship and turn you into each other's biggest fan.

To help your spouse reach his objectives, start with honest and sincere discussions about his aspirations. Understanding his goals, anxieties, and perceived barriers is more important in this conversation than trying to force your expectations upon him. It's about listening—truly, empathetically, and without passing judgment.

Second, creating an atmosphere that inspires your spouse to pursue his goals is critical. It may be as easy as setting out particular hours of the week for him to focus on his projects, or it could be more complex, like attending seminars and workshops that interest him. Your participation and interest in his endeavors demonstrate your backing and confidence in his talents.

Furthermore, it's critical to commemorate each accomplishment, no matter how tiny. Recognizing the little victories along the way inspires confidence and drive in a society that frequently waits for the big ones. Every success is worthy of acknowledgment, whether finishing a certification program, hitting a fitness objective, or committing to a new habit for a month.

The ability to overcome obstacles is just as crucial. Goal achievement is a challenging journey. There will be difficulties; occasionally, your spouse may err or even fail. Your function as a helpful husband is most evident during these times. Failings can be turned into positive learning experiences by providing a shoulder to cry on, analyzing what went wrong, and working together to plan the next steps.

Finally, remember that pursuing goals involves more than simply the final destination—the trip is just as important. It's about developing your resilience, the personal growth you've undergone, and the relationship you've reinforced with your spouse. You'll discover that as you help him achieve his goals, his happiness and health will increase, and so will the caliber and depth of your connection.

Encouraging your spouse to reach their goals and lead a healthy lifestyle is like adding color, texture, and strength to the beautiful fabric of a marriage. Pursuing objectives together shapes you into partners, navigating life's ups and downs with love, support, and respect. It's about more than simply the goals themselves.

Chapter Summary

"Help Him Achieve His Goals" explores how important a spouse is in supporting her partner's goals, both personal and professional. The chapter illustrates the significant impact of believing in and supporting one's spouse, John and Sandra's tale, in turning personal goals into joint triumphs. It highlights the value of having sincere discussions, fostering an encouraging atmosphere, commemorating each accomplishment, responding positively to setbacks, and appreciating the process of pursuing goals. This method strengthens and fortifies the marriage link while promoting personal development and fulfilment.

Important Points

Supporting Your Spouse's Goals: It is important to encourage your partner's aspirations, realising that doing so can greatly improve your relationship's quality and increase their sense of fulfilment.

Understanding and Communication: The value of honest, open communication regarding objectives, worries, and roadblocks and the requirement of listening to others with empathy and without passing judgment.

Establishing a Supportive Environment: One way to create an environment that encourages goal pursuit is to make time for your partner's projects or participate in activities that suit their interests.

Celebrating Successes: Recognising and celebrating any accomplishment, no matter how minor, is critical for increasing self-esteem and motivation.

Navigating Setbacks: How to help your spouse overcome obstacles and setbacks so they can be used as teaching moments and chances for personal development.

Important Takeaways

Supporting One Another's Ambitions: This chapter demonstrates how a partnership can go beyond passion and cultivate a more profound bond and mutual regard.

Active Participation: It's important to show your spouse that you support and believe in their skills by actively participating in their endeavours and showing real interest in them.

Empathy in Communication: To truly understand your partner's goals, you must be open and empathetic to the point where it fortifies the foundation of your connection.

The Power of Tiny Victories: Maintaining momentum and excitement toward bigger goals requires acknowledging and appreciating tiny victories.

Resilience Through Support: The chapter emphasises the value of resilience in both personal development and the strength of the marriage bond by highlighting the critical role that a supportive spouse can play in helping a partner overcome obstacles.

Practical Exercises

Establish a specific time to discuss each other's hopes, worries, and possible roadblocks to create a supportive and judgment-free atmosphere.

Together, create a vision board that symbolises your mutual support and individual aspirations. "This will be a visual representation of the promise and commitment you have made to each other."

Establish weekly check-ins to provide continued communication and support by discussing goals' progress, difficulties, and necessary modifications.

Party Schedule: Schedule occasions to recognise and honour accomplishments, even minor ones, to foster a culture of gratitude and inspiration.

Attend a session or activity centred on developing resilience to improve your ability to collectively deal with setbacks and learn from mistakes.

Reflection Time

How can I foster an environment that is more supportive of my spouse's goals?

___
___
___
___
___
___
___
___
___
___
___
___

What worries or barriers to achieving their goals does my partner see, and how can we jointly address them?

___
___
___
___
___
___

Samantha Nunez Chapman

How can I be genuinely interested in and involved in my spouse's activities without going too far?

Does our definition of success in a relationship reflect our individual and common values? How do we recognise and celebrate it?

How can we turn failures into positive teaching moments that build our resilience as a couple and as individuals?

CHAPTER NINETEEN

Rise And Shine Before He Does

In the vast field of marital advice, rising and gleaming before your mate may seem like a minor, perhaps even insignificant, habit. However, this seemingly straightforward action has essential ramifications for maintaining and growing a robust and happy relationship. When used carefully, this tactic can turn the morning's gloom into a blank canvas of possibility, creating a pleasant vibe for the rest of the day.

Before the day's obligations demand attention, early morning silence provides a unique opportunity for introspection and thought. During these calm initial moments, a mindset centred around the health of the marriage can be developed. You give yourself more time in the morning to do self-improvement activities like reading, meditation, or just sipping tea. This private time is about getting ready to be present and involved with your partner all day, not isolating yourself for selfish purposes.

Additionally, you can set up such an environment with this technique that your lover wakes up to a day warmed by your thoughtfulness and love. Think about the contrast between waking up to an alarm that goes off suddenly and gently rising to find your partner up and about, maybe with the smell of breakfast in the air or the sight of a clean living area. These modest actions go a long way towards creating a sense of care, value, and respect.

Breaking this habit also allows you to surprise your significant other with thoughtful gestures. A kind note on the bathroom mirror, a cooked breakfast, or a warm smile can brighten your partner's day. These deeds of compassion are the strands that bind a married couple's closeness and connection together.

Practically speaking, during this time, you can also review timetables, make plans for the next day, or discuss objectives and aspirations for the day without being disturbed by the turmoil that frequently accompanies the morning rush. It's an opportunity to ensure that you are operating as a team by coordinating what the day has in store for you both.

Understanding that this practice is about striking a balance that works for your relationship rather than giving up on your sleep or your partner's wellbeing is crucial. It could entail changing your bedtime routine to ensure you get enough sleep or talking to your partner about essential ways you can reciprocate this practice.

Being the first to rise and shine before he does symbolises a proactive, considerate, and loving marriage. It's evidence that the saying "it's the little things that count" is true, showing that small, everyday actions of love, care, and cooperation make a marriage strong rather than significant, showy gestures.

This chapter is not just about getting up early; it's also about seizing the chance to strengthen your bond with your significant other. It's deciding to begin each day to foster your relationship and prove to your partner that their happiness and wellbeing come first. In the end, these deliberate moments and everyday reaffirmations of devotion create an indestructible link between spouses in a marriage.

You are getting up before your spouse offers a great chance to start the day pleasantly, particularly regarding marriages. This seemingly small deed can significantly impact the dynamics of your relationship by encouraging self-improvement, independence, and self-care that you and your partner can both benefit from.

Starting your day early gives you time for introspection and isolation. You may experience the serenity and clarity that come from spending time alone with your thoughts in the calm of the early morning, which helps to emotionally and psychologically prepare you for the day. You can use this time to read, practice meditation, or indulge in a hobby that you might not get to do later in the day. These are crucial times for personal growth since they make you happier and more fulfilled, which benefits your marriage.

Additionally, this exercise can significantly improve your organisational abilities and productivity. By rising earlier, you may spend more time organising and setting priorities for your work without feeling rushed or under pressure to get everything done right away when you wake up next to your partner. It's an excellent opportunity to plan your day, make goals, and get ready to surprise your significant other, all of which will deepen your bond.

As a practical tip, try setting your alarm for no more than thirty to sixty minutes before your partner's. Make the most of this time by doing things that uplift your spirits and prepare you for the day. It could be as easy as taking a quiet sip of tea, writing down your ideas or daily to-do list, or doing some yoga. Finding something that personally speaks to you is essential since it will improve your wellbeing and, consequently, the state of your marriage.

From a practical standpoint, consider the tale of Emma and Alex, who discovered that their mornings were hurried and disorganised, frequently resulting in conflicts and annoyance. Gloria decided to begin waking up before Brian, which significantly affected their relationship. She took advantage of the extra time to make a nutritious breakfast for the two of them, something their busy schedules had prevented them from doing. This thoughtful and compassionate deed enhanced their health. It gave them a great start to the day by reestablishing communication and connection previously lost to the morning hustle.

It's crucial to remember that waking up early shouldn't mean compromising your health by getting less sleep. Make sure you get to bed early enough to receive the required 7-9 hours of sleep, as not getting enough sleep can undermine the benefits of this practice by negatively affecting your mood, productivity, and general health.

In summary, you are getting up before your spouse is a strong but frequently disregarded strategy to improve your marriage. It gives you valuable time for personal development and self-care, allows you to plan and organise your day, and enables you to show your spouse kindness, deepening your bond. Recall that making the most of this time together as a couple and individually means more than simply getting up early.

Chapter Summary

"Rise and Shine Before He Does" explores the subtle but significant effects of rising earlier in the day on a marriage's well-being than your spouse's. This chapter explains how this seemingly easy behaviour may create a loving atmosphere, encourage self-improvement, and strengthen the relationship's mutual respect and caring. It makes the case that the early hours provide a special opportunity for reflection, preparation, and carrying out kind deeds that greatly strengthen a marriage. This chapter promotes using the peace of daybreak to strengthen the relationship through doable suggestions and accessible examples, stressing the significance of balance and mutual understanding in this practice.

Important Points

Reflection in the Morning: Using the peacefulness of the early hours of the day to work on oneself promotes personal development and prepares one to be more attentive and involved in the relationship all day.

Putting Together a Comfortable Wake-Up Setting: Make your partner feel loved, cared for, and appreciated by creating a cosy and welcoming morning atmosphere. It will make a big difference in their day.

Sensible Motions Strengthen Bond: In the morning, small gestures of generosity, such as making breakfast or leaving a note, can make a big impression and enhance the emotional connection.

Chance for Planning and Coordination: To guarantee that a couple functions as a cohesive unit, mornings can be a great time to talk and synchronise their plans and schedules.

Find a balance that honours the needs of both partners: The practice suggests making adaptations, such as changing nighttime rituals to guarantee adequate rest.

Important Takeaways

The transformative power of routine: Regular behaviours can strengthen relationships. For example, a seemingly insignificant habit like getting up early in the morning can significantly impact marital harmony.

Self-Care as Marital Care: Making improvements to oneself and taking care of oneself helps the person and strengthens the marriage by creating a happier, more contented partner.

Thoughtful morning gestures are effective nonverbal communication methods that convey love, gratitude, and commitment to one's spouse and relationship.

The Value of Synchronicity: Keeping daily schedules and objectives in line can greatly improve a couple's collaboration and cooperation by creating chances for connection, even in the most ordinary tasks.

Personalisation and Adaptability: The success of waking up early in a relationship hinge on how well it fits the couple's particular dynamics, emphasising the significance of tailoring marital counsel to each couple.

Practical Exercises

Morning Reflection Journal: Write your thoughts, feelings, and aspirations for the day in your journal for the first ten minutes after waking up. Concentrate on how you might strengthen your marriage.

Breakfast Surprise: Make your significant other a special breakfast once a week to show them how much you care and to begin their day with love and gratitude.

Together, plan your daily routine and goals for the day, spending a few minutes in the morning discussing how you may best support one another's efforts.

Nighttime Adjustment Plan: Together, modify your nighttime schedule to ensure that you receive enough sleep and that getting up early is advantageous for both of you.

Weekly Gesture Challenge: To keep the practice meaningful and fresh, set a weekly goal for yourself to think of a new, tiny act of kindness or surprise your partner in the morning.

Reflection Time

How does making time in the morning for reflection and personal development impact your involvement and presence in your relationship?

_____
_____
_____
_____
_____
_____
_____
_____
_____
_____
_____
_____

How do kind deeds in the morning strengthen and deepen your marital bond?

_____
_____
_____
_____
_____

How can you show your lover how much you care and appreciate them by making their morning pleasant?

How important is it for you and your spouse to align your goals and schedules, and how does this practice impact your feeling of collaboration?

Samantha Nunez Chapman

_____
_____
_____
_____

Think about balancing your partner's and your time in the morning. How do you ensure this is a mutually beneficial practice without sacrificing your health?

_____
_____
_____
_____
_____
_____
_____
_____
_____
_____
_____
_____
_____

CHAPTER TWENTY

Encourage Him to Maintain a Healthy Lifestyle

IN THE MOSAIC OF MARRIAGE, SUPPORTING ONE'S SPOUSE to lead healthy lifestyle weaves together love, worry, and the goal of shared longevity. This act entails fostering an environment where both partners feel motivated to achieve their best selves, intellectually and physically, and it goes beyond simple recommendations for eating healthily or exercising.

The foundation for this endeavour lays the knowledge that leading a healthy lifestyle is a journey rather than a destination—one that is immensely more pleasurable and feasible when shared with someone you love. This chapter offers helpful guidance on fostering this shared journey with sensitivity, creativity, and a strong sense of collaboration for newlyweds, eager learners, seasoned spouses, and those committed to improving their relationships.

Above all, it's critical to understand that there are various sorts of support and that what works for one couple might not be appropriate for another. Therefore, it's critical to take a customised approach that considers the particular dynamics of your relationship and the personalities of the individuals involved.

Participating in activities both spouses enjoy could be a sensible place to start. Shared activities, like taking a brisk stroll in the park, taking a dance class, or cooking a new, healthful cuisine together, encourage a healthy lifestyle and deepen the link between partners. These happy times spent together can act as a vital source of motivation, transforming what could otherwise be considered a chore into a part of your routine that you look forward to.

Furthermore, it can be prosperous to create shared objectives. These objectives don't have to be enormous; modest, attainable goals are frequently more motivating because they provide the instant gratification of achievement. No matter how tiny, celebrate these wins with one another since they are all steps towards living a better life.

Encouragement language is also critical. It should always be uplifting, encouraging, and judgment-free. Sayings such as "I feel so good when we cook healthy meals together" or "I'm really proud of us for taking that walk, even though it was raining" highlight the positive experiences and deeds rather than portraying the change in lifestyle as a solution to an issue. This positive reinforcement strengthens the link between healthy behaviours and emotional intimacy, increasing lifestyle modifications' desirability.

Partners may occasionally differ in their drive or enthusiasm to lead healthy lives. It's crucial to be patient and empathetic in these situations. Persuasion should never be associated with encouragement. Instead, work to identify the underlying cause of any resistance and jointly address it. One partner may fear the other's superior fitness or health expertise. Learning together can be a great tactic in this situation because it makes both partners feel vulnerable and fosters growth.

Furthermore, achieving mental and emotional well-being is a necessary part of the path to a healthy lifestyle. Encouraging your spouse to openly discuss their emotions, worries, and anxieties without fear of rejection can improve your relationship emotionally and lay the groundwork for good physical health. The concept that mental health is equally important to physical health can be reinforced by exploring stress-reduction techniques like yoga, meditation, and basic mindfulness exercises.

In summary, supporting your significant other to lead a healthy lifestyle shows love and devotion. Building a life together where both partners feel appreciated, encouraged, and motivated to be their best selves is more important than simply following a diet and exercising. Couples can start this journey together and fortify their marriage in significant and long-lasting ways by concentrating on shared activities, setting realistic goals, having a constructive and encouraging conversation, and attending to physical and emotional well-being.

Keep His Secrets

Maintaining one's partner's secrets is a sign of safety and a foundation of trust in the marriage sphere. It is impossible to emphasise how important this idea is to the structure of a happy marriage. When we talk about secrets, we don't mean to keep lousy information to ourselves; instead, we mean to protect our partner's private ideas, anxieties, and dreams. This chapter explores the subtleties and significant effects of maintaining secrets inside the sacred boundaries of marriage, focusing on how to do so while forging a more vital link between partners.

The idea of trust is fundamental to maintaining secrets. Trust is the sensitive but vital cornerstone of any relationship, and it is particularly important in marriage. Your partner's trust in your empathy and understanding is demonstrated when they confide in you. This gesture expresses, "I trust you with the parts of me that the outside world doesn't see." You are silently pledging to respect and value their vulnerabilities by keeping their secrets private.

However, this work can occasionally be difficult due to the complexity of human emotions and events. It's critical to distinguish between maintaining secrets that could damage a marriage and innocuous and intimate ones. The former concerns details like financial difficulties or infidelity that, if kept secret, could compromise the integrity of the relationship. The latter concerns ideas or memories that, however delicate and intimate, do not directly affect the state of the relationship. Here, the emphasis is on keeping these innocuous secrets private to increase confidence.

Active listening is a valuable strategy for becoming proficient in this skill. When your significant other opens up about something personal, listen without interrupting to comprehend. They feel appreciated and respected when you empathise with them, creating a safe space for transparency. Determining the level of sensitivity of the transmitted information is also crucial. Consider the question, "Is this something my partner would want others to know?" Keep it confidential and err on the side of caution if you're not sure.

In many instances in real life, maintaining secrets has strengthened bonds with others. Think about the tale of Anna and Liam (names withheld for privacy), who disclosed all details to one another, including Liam's anxiety issues. Understanding Liam's right to privacy and his concern about criticism from friends and family, Anna decided to keep this to herself. This choice strengthened their relationship, as Liam felt comfortable knowing that Anna would protect his weaknesses. These exchanges of empathy and support in silence highlight the importance of protecting secrets.

Furthermore, maintaining confidentiality involves more than simply the act itself; it also entails fostering an environment of respect and understanding between parties. When you do this, you become your partner's confidante and safe haven. This promotes a stronger emotional connection and fortifies the marriage.

Maintaining your partner's confidentiality is a powerful sign of respect and trust in a married relationship. It's about defending their weak points and strengthening the intimacy and security that are the cornerstones of your partnership. Recall that a marriage's strength comes from the secrets that are securely held close to the vest and the shared joys. Embracing this principle as newlyweds, eager learners, seasoned spouses, and relationship enhancers is essential to fostering long-lasting, loving relationships.

Chapter Summary

Promoting a healthy lifestyle and showing consideration for your partner's privacy. The first section emphasises the importance of collaboration, support, and innovation in promoting a partnership's mental and physical health. It highlights that maintaining a healthy lifestyle requires collaboration and offers specific guidance, such as having fun together, setting reasonable goals, and never stopping to offer encouragement. The second part of the article discusses the profound implications of trust and privacy in relationships, highlighting the delicate balance between protecting your partner's secrets and not disclosing them. It illustrates how closeness and trust are strengthened in marriages by upholding personal space and showing your partner care.

Important Points

Promoting a Healthier Lifestyle Collectively: Creating an atmosphere where both couples are driven to live a healthy lifestyle improves the individual's health and the stability of the marriage.

Customisation and Shared Activities: The key to making the journey towards health fun and sustainable is identifying activities that both couples love and creating realistic shared goals.

The Language of Encouragement: Making lifestyle adjustments feel satisfying and linked to emotional closeness requires positive reinforcement and an upbeat tone.

Privacy and Trust: Maintaining your spouse's secrets shows high security and trust in your marriage, strengthens your relationship, and creates a secure environment for you both.

Differentiating Between Harmful and Harmless Secrets: It's important to preserve integrity and trust in marriage by knowing which secrets belong to personal privacy and which could jeopardise the union.

Important Takeaways

Cooperation Rather Than Compulsion: Promoting a healthy lifestyle and keeping secrets are two activities that benefit from cooperation between parties rather than compulsion or pressure.

Emotional Well-Being as the Foundation: Programmes aimed at promoting physical health are more effective when combined with those aimed at enhancing mental and emotional well-being, underscoring the interdependence of wellness.

The Function of Active Listening: By helping you comprehend your partner's needs and boundaries, you can strengthen their confidence in you as a confidante.

Maintaining your partner's secrets is a sign of the sacredness of the marriage, which emphasises the value of privacy in laying a solid foundation of trust. Privacy is paramount.

Common Objectives Promote Closer Bonds: When partners set and accomplish health objectives together, it can greatly strengthen their emotional bond and make every accomplishment a joint achievement.

Practical Exercises

Weekly Activity Planning: Take some time each week to arrange an enjoyable health-related activity for the two of you. Schedule this regularly, whether it's a yoga class, bike ride, or cooking class.

Goal-Setting Session: Together, establish modest, attainable health goals. Consider giving each other a modest gift or organising a special outing to commemorate these milestones.

Encouragement diary: Keep a shared diary in which you can record supportive messages and positive affirmations for one another. The journal should be focused on your health journey and your efforts to uphold confidentiality and trust.

Practice Active Listening: Set aside some weekly time to practice active listening. Exchange intimate details with your companion and take on a new position, listening intently without interjecting or passing judgment.

Establish a privacy agreement by discussing and deciding what information is private in your union. Put these commitments in writing as a reminder of your commitment to respecting each other's privacy.

Reflection Time

How do our shared objectives for individual and combined health compare, and how can we help each other achieve them?

_____
_____
_____
_____
_____
_____
_____
_____
_____
_____
_____
_____

How can we both find enjoyment and fulfilment in our quest towards a better lifestyle?

What does privacy mean to each of us in our relationship, and are there any places where we still need to work on respecting and understanding one another's boundaries?

Samantha Nunez Chapman

Think back to a moment when your significant other revealed something personal to you. What lessons about intimacy and trust in a relationship did it teach you, and how did you respond to it?

_____
_____
_____
_____
_____
_____
_____
_____
_____
_____
_____
_____
_____
_____

How can we enhance each other's well-being and deepen our relationship through positive reinforcement and encouragement?

_____
_____
_____
_____
_____
_____
_____
_____
_____
_____
_____
_____
_____
_____

CHAPTER TWENTY ONE

Before You Say Something Hurtful, Do A Gut Check

MAINTAINING A PRECISE BALANCE BETWEEN EMPATHY AND HONESTY is necessary when navigating the complex web of marital communication. Doing a "gut check" before saying something cruel is a crucial tactic that can turn disagreements into chances for greater understanding and connection. This chapter explores the fundamentals of mindful communication, emphasising the need to pause critically before reacting during tense situations.

The capacity for efficient communication is the foundation of each happy marriage. The problem comes when feelings are strong, and they want to respond with harsh words. In these situations, doing a "gut check" becomes helpful. A "gut check" is a brief pause involving careful consideration of our words' meaning before we speak. It acts as a cushion, enabling us to evaluate our genuine intentions and the possible effects of our words on our relationship.

Imagine if your significant other forgets a big event, like an anniversary or a significant professional achievement. The first reaction could be to express dissatisfaction or displeasure in a way that could be interpreted as offensive. But before you say anything, a "gut check" asks you to think about the following: Is the goal to communicate your thoughts constructively or to cause your partner to feel just as disappointed? By reflecting on oneself, one might adopt a more sympathetic and perceptive stance that invites productive conversation rather than escalating hostilities.

The 'gut check' approach aims to improve empathy and understanding in the context of marriage rather than just censoring. We try to understand our partner's point of view by being mindful of the possible effects of our words and practising empathy. This strategy change can significantly alter the way disputes are settled, fostering an atmosphere of respect and understanding between parties.

Examples of this behaviour in the real world abound. Consider the couple who, during a furious dispute over money, took a moment to reflect on the strains and stresses they were both under. During this reflective time, they were able to move from a point of accusation to one of mutual support, and they were able to come up with a solution that took into account both of their worries.

It takes time and experience to put the "gut check" into practice. Realising that sometimes our first responses might be less beneficial is the first step in the process. By developing the practice of taking a moment to consider our words and their potential consequences, we may make decisions about how to respond that strengthen rather than weaken our marriage.

Furthermore, the 'gut check' is an effective instrument for personal development. It pushes us to face our fears and stressors, which develops our emotional intelligence and self-awareness. This introspective journey strengthens our marriage and advances our personal growth.

The "gut check" is a commitment to fostering a marriage where communication is founded on empathy, understanding, and respect rather than just a brief stop. It is evidence of how mindfulness may turn the inevitable disputes in married life into chances for development and closer relationships. Couples who embrace this approach can cultivate a long-lasting connection built on deep knowledge and respect for one another.

Cook Dinner

In essence, cooking dinner involves much more than just chopping and cooking. Marriage is a fabric that includes threads of compassion, empathy, and gratitude for times spent together. This seemingly small but significant deed proves the caring spirit essential to the journey of companionship.

Just picture coming home to the warm smell of a well-made supper after a day full of obstacles. This is not merely a scenario of feeding hunger; it's a silent dialogue, an attempt to convey, "I care about your well-being," without exchanging words. These are the times when a marriage, which is based on small acts of love like making dinner, is strengthened.

Learning to cook together is like learning a new skill that adds life to the canvas of your married life, whether you are a seasoned couple, a couple searching for adventure, or a married couple with years of experience together. It's about finding flavours that make your partner happy, experimenting with components that tell the tale of your relationship, and making memories that last long after the food is cleared.

Rather than its intricacy, the motive behind preparing a meal gives it power when shared with others. The labour and thinking that goes into making dinner captures the spirit of cooking, whether a three-course meal or a straightforward, comforting dish. It's about setting aside time from our frequently busy lives to concentrate on what counts: strengthening your relationship with your partner.

One way to practically incorporate this into your marriage is to learn about your partner's dietary constraints and preferences. This understanding serves as the basis for your shared gastronomic adventure. Talk about your family's treasured recipes and your favourite childhood dinners, or try out new foods together. These conversations not only broaden your culinary skills but also strengthen your bond.

Additionally, incorporate your cooking partner in the process. This doesn't have to entail constantly having them in the kitchen; it can be as easy as consulting them when selecting meals or letting them help with grocery shopping. These joint choices strengthen the bond between the two people and promote equality and teamwork.

Couples who have discovered that cooking together or for one another has been a joyful discovery process abound in real-life examples. It's about sharing a private meal with loved ones, toasting a cake that turns out just right, or just laughing over a botched effort at a new recipe. Every one of these incidents functions as a cornerstone for a more robust and durable connection.

Additionally, making dinner for your significant other or together might become a haven of quality time in this day and age when time is sometimes a luxury. It's a chance to take a break from technology and have meaningful conversations with people in person. Having this time together to catch up, talk about your day, and make plans for the future is so beneficial.

Essentially, preparing dinner is a microcosm of marriage in general. It takes time, effort, flexibility, and, most of all, love. Let the kitchen serve as your haven as you work to strengthen your marriage. It's a place to express your love, find solace, and create enduring memories with your spouse. By doing this, you not only validate the saying that the path to one's heart does indeed lead via one's stomach, but you also foster the kind of memories and shared experiences around the dinner table.

Despite its seeming simplicity, preparing dinner for a mate may be a profound act of love and participation within the sacred connection of marriage. This act, which has its roots in providing for the body and the soul, is essential to developing an intimate and nurturing shared life. It represents a daily chance to show your partner commitment, empathy, and inventiveness and goes beyond the simple act of cooking.

In the worlds of newlywed bliss, eager learners experienced companionship, and the never-ending path of relationship enhancement; making dinner together or for one another is a sign of a partner's devotion and love. Despite the craziness of everyday life, it's a time when couples may get together, exchange stories, and perform an act of mutual care.

Dinner preparation for individuals starting this path entails more than just following recipes. To better understand one another, learning about and respecting one another's nutritional requirements, tastes, and preferences is essential. Dinner becomes a blank canvas on which you can examine and appreciate the subtleties of both your partner's and your own characters. Whether modifying a dish to accommodate a dietary restriction or adding a cherished component, these decisions represent the flexibility and attentiveness that marriages require.

Preparing dinner for your partner or jointly is a practical way to represent the values of cooperation and teamwork. It's a planning, teamwork, and responsibility-sharing activity. Selecting a meal, grocery shopping, and assigning culinary duties to different people, all help improve collaboration and communication. This shared experience may turn a mundane chore into a happy occasion to celebrate your marriage, transforming the kitchen into a hub for love, laughter, and education.

Cooking dinner also serves as a powerful reminder of the value of setting aside time for one another to stop and enjoy small but meaningful moments. In today's fast-paced world, when time is frequently scarce, making an effort to cook dinner represents placing your partnership above all the demands of life. Deciding to spend quality time together strengthens your marriage bond with each meal.

Practically speaking, cooking at home provides both parties the chance to live a better lifestyle, a mutually beneficial objective. Cooking can become a wellness adventure where you try new, nourishing meals to help you both live long, healthy lives. It's an investment in your future and a sign of your concern for one another's well-being.

When incorporating cooking into your married life, remember to accept the setbacks and flaws that occur. Every burned dish and imperfect dinner is an opportunity for learning, laughing, and team development. These are the times when your relationship is put to the test and strengthened, and when you may enjoy the beauty of your shared imperfections.

It's essential to approach cooking dinner with an open heart and mind if you want to use it to build your marriage genuinely. Try new foods, tell the backstories of your favourite dishes, and establish new customs to enhance your married life. At its core, this simple gesture becomes a daily reaffirmation of your commitment to care for, love, and support one another during good times and bad.

To sum up, preparing dinner is more than just setting the table with food. It's about the love it symbolises, the hands that prepare it, and the hearts that share it. It's a way to show each other daily how much you care, support, and love each other. As such, it is a crucial yet remarkably straightforward foundation of a happy marriage.

Chapter Summary

The significance of mindful communication through "Before You Say Something Hurtful, Do A Gut Check" and the symbolic act of love of preparing dinner for your spouse are two important components of married life. Both parts strongly emphasise understanding, empathy, and the little but important things that make a marriage stronger. You are urged to develop a stronger connection with your spouse by practising mindfulness in your words and deeds and participating in loving activities like cooking together through helpful guidance and real-world examples. These behaviours are about fostering a kind, courteous, and loving relationship—not only about avoiding confrontation or providing for one another.

Important Points

Mindful Communication: This approach promotes empathy and understanding above damaging words by highlighting the importance of doing a "gut check" before speaking during arguments.

Empathy in Action: This shows how letting our words affect others can turn possible confrontations into opportunities for development and communication.

Making dinner for or with your lover is a significant act of care that strengthens your bond even when you're not together at the dinner table.

Shared Experiences: Promotes cooking as a means for couples to strengthen their relationship, understand one another's preferences more, and create enduring memories.

Personal Development and Emotional Intelligence: The significance of self-awareness, emotional intelligence, and personal development in strengthening a marriage is emphasised in both segments.

Important Takeaways

Speaking Without Words: Effective marital communication, according to the "gut check" method, is about expressing respect, understanding, and love even when no words are spoken.

Empathy as a Foundation: Since empathy strengthens an emotional bond between partners, it makes navigating obstacles in a marriage easier, especially for married couples.

Actions frequently speak louder than words, as evidenced by the power of simple gestures like making dinner. These gestures can have a tremendous effect on a relationship.

Cooking Together: Cooking together is a great way to create rituals and shared meanings that improve the marriage and nourish the body.

Growth via Reflection: Promoting emotional intelligence and self-reflection furthers personal development, which benefits a happier, healthier marriage.

Practical Exercises

Establishing a "Gut Check" Routine: This week, try pausing before answering disagreements. Consider how this affects the outcome of disputes.

Organise and carry out a cooking date night in which you both help prepare a meal. Think back on the incident and the lessons it imparted to your spouse.

Dinner and Conversation: Take this opportunity to have in-depth discussions. Select significant themes for your relationship and discuss them while enjoying the meal you prepared together.

Weekly Recipe Swap: Exchange your best recipes from your earliest years or single life. While cooking the dish together, tell each other stories related to it.

Keep a thankfulness diary: Begin by keeping a thankfulness diary in which you both record daily compliments and acts of kindness, such as cooking or considerate conversation.

Reflection Time

How does your communication change when you conduct a "gut check" before answering during a heated moment?

_____
_____
_____
_____
_____
_____
_____
_____
_____
_____
_____
_____
_____

Beyond simply sharing meals, how does cooking for or with your partner strengthen your bond?

_____
_____
_____

Samantha Nunez Chapman

When was the last time you felt that a small gesture of kindness, like making your partner dinner with care, greatly influenced your relationship?

How do mindful communication techniques and bonding activities like cooking affect your development as a couple?

Samantha Nunez Chapman

Consider how adopting these routines has changed how you handle conflict and maintain your relationship. What changes have you observed?

CHAPTER TEWNTY TWO

Take His Mother Out to Lunch

CREATING DEEP CONNECTIONS WITH EACH OTHER'S FAMILIES, especially the in-laws, is another important aspect of navigating the complex dance of marriage that frequently involves more than just the two spouses. Of all these relationships, the one between a wife and her husband's mother is particularly important. This chapter explores the profound effects on your marriage and the more significant dynamics of the family that can result from taking your husband's mother out to lunch.

Going to lunch with your husband's mother is an opportunity to do more than share a meal; it's also a chance to strengthen bonds and broaden understanding. It's a kind gesture that shows your regard and commitment to this vital partnership. Such behaviours are fundamental to building a happy family environment and a sense of cohesion and acceptance.

This could seem like a big step for a newlywed couple, mainly if you're still settling into your new family. However, these initial attempts have the power to determine how the connection develops in the future. This gesture can also be valuable to seasoned spouses, as it revitalises long-standing relationships and reaffirms their dedication to family harmony.

When organising this meal, take into account her interests and preferences. Selecting a dining establishment or menu that she likes is a way to show her that you appreciate her comfort and happiness. These little things can have a significant impact by demonstrating your attention to detail and concern for her well-being.

Lunchtime conversations should strive to be inclusive and exciting. This is a great chance to learn more about your husband's childhood, background, and any family customs his mother might hold dear. By revealing shared interests, sharing experiences and tales can also help close any communication gaps. It's crucial to use this time to actively listen and demonstrate that you genuinely care about what she has to say. Building trust and empathy, two vital elements of any healthy relationship, may be accomplished mainly by listening.

Additionally, you can improve your husband's opinion of your relationship by bringing his mother out to lunch. It strengthens the partnership element of your marriage by displaying your dedication to becoming an essential family member. Your spouse will likely feel proud of you and grateful for your attempts to establish a closer connection with his family as a result of these acts.

But it's essential to go into this meal without preconceived notions of what kind of change you want. Relationships take time to develop, and the accumulation of these little acts of kindness progressively strengthens the link. Navigating the intricacies of in-law relationships requires perseverance, patience, and a positive outlook.

To sum up, a small gesture like taking your husband's mother to lunch can significantly impact your marriage and family dynamics. It's a gesture of deference, an investment in maintaining family unity, and a move toward a shared future. By accepting this opportunity with an open heart and mind, you can create a more accepting and loving family atmosphere and strengthen your marriage. Recall that these threads of respect and connection combine to form a larger, more vibrant picture in the magnificent tapestry of marriage.

Chapter Summary

This chapter explores the significance of building solid family bonds, especially between a wife and her husband's mother. It emphasises the significant influence that extending an invitation to your husband's mother for lunch can have on your marriage and family dynamics. This gesture is about more than just sharing a meal; it's about expressing respect, strengthening relationships, and committing to maintaining family unity. This small act of kindness can greatly improve empathy, understanding, and trust in the family via careful planning and meaningful dialogue, bolstering the marriage and fostering a peaceful home atmosphere.

Important Points

Importance of In-Law Relationships: A wife's harmony and happiness within the family greatly depend on her relationship with her husband's mother. Here, a good rapport can greatly impact marital and larger family relationships.

The gesture of Goodwill: Treating your husband's mother to lunch is a concrete way to show your appreciation and dedication to preserving the family dynamic. It's an investment in the happiness and unity of the family for the future.

Personalisation and thoughtfulness: Choosing a meal and venue that suits her tastes shows that you've thought about everything and are concerned about her comfort, strengthening your relationship.

Possibility for Improved Communication: By giving people a forum to share interests, experiences, and family customs over lunch, communication gaps can be filled, and mutual understanding and trust can be developed.

Favourable Effect on Marriage: Demonstrating your commitment to your husband's family can positively impact your relationship.

Important Takeaways

Establishing Trust with Active Listening: During these exchanges, active listening is critical to fostering trust and empathy, two essentials for any successful partnership.

Relationships, particularly those with in-laws, are built incrementally through good deeds, emphasising the value of endurance and forbearance.

The Role of Gestures in Family Dynamics: Seemingly small actions, For instance, consider inviting someone to have lunch together., can greatly impact the quality of marriage ties and family dynamics.

Cultural and own Sensitivity: Showing the family that you genuinely care about and are committed to them requires that you comprehend and respect their traditions and choices.

Avoiding Preconceived Expectations: By entering these kinds of conversations without preconceived notions, relationships are free to develop organically, leading to a more genuine and meaningful connection.

Practical Exercises

Arrange a Surprise Lunch: Show your mother-in-law that you've given it some thought by looking into and selecting a location that suits her preferences.

Family Traditions Quiz: Before the meal, list questions about customs, tales, or your spouse's early years to promote conversation and camaraderie.

Active Listening Challenge: Practice active listening during lunch by paying close attention to what your mother-in-law says and refraining from interrupting or planning your response.

Follow-Up Gesture: Send a handwritten note expressing appreciation for your time together over lunch, emphasising a particular incident or tale discussed.

Journal Reflection: After lunch, write in your journal about the event, jotting down any new information you learned about your husband's family and suggestions for strengthening your bonds with them.

Reflection Time

Why, in your opinion, is a harmonious connection with your husband's mother essential to the family?

___
___
___
___
___
___
___
___
___
___
___
___

How can you show your husband's family that you genuinely care about them in addition to simply asking them to lunch?

___
___
___

Samantha Nunez Chapman

How can you learn more about your spouse's family history on these outings by paying attention and having meaningful conversations?

Think back to any early concerns you may have had about asking your mother-in-law to lunch. How did your expectations and the real world differ?

Samantha Nunez Chapman

How can you use the knowledge you've gained from this lunch to improve your bonds with your family members and foster a welcoming, caring environment?

CHAPTER TWENTY-THREE

Be Your Man's Best Friend

STARTING A MARRIED LIFE FREQUENTLY UNFOLDS LIKE A MAP to unknown territory, with companionship's landscape ranging from the comfortably predictable to the untamedly unexpected. One of the most important things you can do in the complex dance of married life is genuinely become your partner's best friend. This idea, the foundation of a happy partnership, acts as a lighthouse to help us navigate life's challenges together.

It's not just about the happy times you had laughing beneath the sun or the same hobbies that drew you together to become your man's best friend. It goes far beyond into the domain of profound understanding, support, and connection that endures life's storms. It's about building a solid foundation in which love and comfort are felt as strongly as a summer breeze, even in the quiet.

To nurture this unique connection within your marriage, start by thinking about what it truly means to be someone's best friend. Fundamentally, this position is based on a foundation of open communication, trust, and the uncommon capacity to provide space when needed. It necessitates an appreciation that although romance binds you together, the power of your friendship will sustain your partnership through all of life's phases.

Vulnerability and Trust

Trust is a vital component of every meaningful relationship, and it becomes even more important when you want to be your husband's best friend. It's the assurance that when one shares one's vulnerabilities, one will be greeted with compassion and understanding rather than condemnation. Maintaining this degree of trust requires you to be truthful in your words and deeds. Recall that trust is about being a trustworthy confidante for both big and small ambitions, not only about being faithful.

Assistance Across the Spectrum

You can provide your partner emotional, intellectual, and occasionally physical support. It's being there for people in happy times and lending support when things get tough. Crucially, support also entails encouraging them to pursue their goals and personal development, even if they differ from yours. This could include supporting pastimes or interests you don't share or acknowledging accomplishments you don't entirely get but know are significant to him.

Conversation: The Vital Signs of Companionship

Communication in friendship, particularly in marriage, goes beyond the routine banter about everyday activities. It entails disclosing your most private aspirations, anxieties, and desires. It's about treating one another with care and respect during those difficult talks, even when you don't agree. Listening is just as crucial to effective communication as speaking. Friendships are strengthened when one partner feels heard and seen, and this is achieved through listening with the intention of understanding rather than responding.

The Space Gift

There's a delicate balance between connection and individualism in every close relationship. Your partner can refuel and keep their sense of self when you respect their desire for space. Realising that taking time for yourself doesn't mean your relationship is in danger—instead, it might strengthen it. You can show your spouse that you trust and feel secure in the relationship by encouraging them to follow their hobbies or spend time with friends.

Common Experiences and Recollections

Creating a private language of shared experiences and memories is similar to building a treasure trove. When you reflect on these times, they remind you of the adventure you have taken together. These encounters strengthen and strengthen your bond, whether they are planned excursions or the development of traditions.

Compassion and Pardoning

Empathy enables you to put yourself in your partner's position, experience their emotions, and comprehend their viewpoint. When combined with forgiveness, it fosters a culture where errors are seen as learning experiences rather than grounds for punishment. It's admitting that each other's imperfections are imperfect and that grace should be our default reaction. Perfection is a myth.

Being your partner's best friend is a theme that runs across every part of your life, not just a chapter in the magnificent tapestry of marriage. It's the unspoken pledge to support, share laughs and tears, encourage and confront one another, fall madly in love, and live life to the fullest. Let the pursuit of this deep friendship be the light that leads you, the strength that holds you up, and the joy that permeates your days as you navigate the lovely complexities of marriage.

Chapter Summary

"Be Your Man's Best Friend" captures the spirit of creating a strong, meaningful relationship in a marriage, drawing comparisons to the deep friendship between true friends. It emphasises the value of open communication, trust, support from one another, and shared experiences as the cornerstones of a friendship that goes beyond passionate love to exemplify the traits of best friends. This chapter sheds light on the journey of married life. It promotes a friendship that grows out of empathy, understanding, and striking a balance between one's individuality and unity, all of which build a strong, happy marriage.

Important Points

Deep Understanding and Support: Being your partner's closest friend mostly depends on having a solid understanding of them and providing them with constant support despite life's unpredictable events.

Trust and Vulnerability: It's critical to create a safe environment where both partners may freely express their deepest worries, hopes, and dreams without fear of repercussions.

Effective Listening and Communication: Listening and sharing each other's deepest hopes and worries with empathy and respect goes beyond casual chats.

Maintaining Individuality and Togetherness: Respecting each partner's desire for privacy in the relationship helps them be true to themselves and their interests, which strengthens the bond between them.

Shared Memories: Establishing a storehouse of shared memories and experiences strengthens the tie between partners and improves friendship and camaraderie in marriage.

Important Takeaways

Friendship as the Foundation of Marriage: The chapter highlights how important companionship is in overcoming obstacles in marriage by revealing that the strength of marriage frequently rests in the underlying friendship between spouses.

The Importance of Empathy and Forgiveness: It is emphasised that empathy and forgiveness are essential elements of a happy marriage in which errors are seen as learning experiences rather than causes for contention.

The Value of Personal Development: Mutual respect and marital progress are fostered when partners support one another's interests and personal development, even when they diverge.

Establishing a Culture of Trust: Trust is not just about faithfulness but also about being dependable and transparent, fostering a strong sense of friendship.

The Importance of Developing Customs: Having common rituals and customs strengthens the marriage by giving the couple a feeling of continuity and identity.

Practical Exercises

Weekly Trust Talks: To build a stronger level of trust, set aside some time each week to share with your partner something intimate or vulnerable that you haven't before disclosed.

Interest Swap: In this exchange, each partner choose a pastime or activity they both enjoy but are not very knowledgeable about. Together, spend a day engaging in these pursuits, demonstrating your support and curiosity for one another's interests.

Listening Sessions: Establish a "no-interruption" policy and limit your interruptions to learning your partner's point of view when talking about your goals, worries, or hopes.

Make a Memory Bank: Gather your best memories and adventures into a scrapbook or digital album, and add to it after every big journey or occasion.

Establish a day, called "Space Day," when everyone spends time exploring their own hobbies, either by themselves or with friends. Get together again to discuss your observations and experiences from the day.

Reflection Time

How can I proactively demonstrate that I appreciate and encourage my husband's goals and aspirations?

_____
_____
_____
_____
_____
_____
_____
_____
_____
_____
_____
_____
_____

When my husband discloses something sensitive, how should I react? Does my response promote more transparency?

Samantha Nunez Chapman

Are there any communication gaps that need to be filled to strengthen our bond and friendship?

How can we better encourage one other's personal development and strike a balance between our time together and our unique interests?

What brand-new custom or activity can we add to our marriage to deepen our relationship and connection?

Samantha Nunez Chapman

CHAPTER TWENTY-FOUR

Making Time for Him

MAKING TIME FOR YOUR PARTNER IS MORE THAN JUST FINDING minutes in your hectic schedule; it involves putting your relationship's emotional and psychological health first despite the clamour of life's obligations. In the context of marriage, spending time with your spouse goes beyond the mundane importance of quality time spent together; it indicates how much you cherish your relationship.

In the modern world, where personal goals and work obligations frequently take precedence over the simple pleasures of a healthy relationship, the importance of deliberately making time for your partner cannot be emphasised enough. This choice reflects the depth of your commitment and the importance of your shared happiness as a symbol and a practical measure.

Comprehending the Temporal Structure of Marriage

Time is a complex concept in a married relationship. Stronger ties are created not only by the quantity of time spent together but also by the calibre and purpose of those times. Making time for meaningful conversations, engaging in similar interests, and being in the moment together can all lead to a deeper, more intimate connection.

Consider the difference, for example, between spending time together in the same room while engrossed in your electronic gadgets and putting those distractions aside to have a meaningful conversation about your day, your dreams, or simply the little things in life. The latter is, without a doubt, a more profound expression of spending time together, emphasising the relationship's spiritual and emotional growth.

Useful Time-Management Techniques

Active Scheduling: It's a sensible strategy to deliberately set aside time for your spouse during the hectic daily grind. This suggests gently prioritising shared experiences rather than the formality of business interactions. The secret is consistency and mutual understanding of the significance of these times, whether it's a weekly session to dream and plan, an evening on the town, or a morning stroll.

Digital detox: In a time when screens rule our lives, choosing to disconnect and concentrate on one another can be a very effective way to strengthen relationships. Set up specific times or areas in your house as technology-free zones so that you and your partner can communicate without being distracted by devices and notifications all the time.

Quality over Quantity: Spending quality time with your spouse is more important than spending time together because of the depth of connection you create throughout these exchanges. A few minutes of your attention and sincere conversation will strengthen your bond.

Shared Experiences: Spending time with someone who enjoys the same activities or hobbies can make the time together more meaningful. Cooking, hiking, or taking up new hobbies are examples of shared activities that can promote camaraderie and teamwork.

Comprehending and Adaptable: The time each pair needs for one another may differ. It's critical to be tolerant of these requirements and to have an honest conversation about them. Making time for your partner occasionally entails allowing them to pursue their interests and realising that relationship health is influenced by personal development.

Samantha Nunez Chapman

The Aftereffects of Scheduling Time

Making time for your spouse provides benefits that go well beyond the happiness that comes from spending time together. It improves communication, fortifies the basis of respect and trust, and creates a storehouse of joyful memories that may be a source of support during trying times. Furthermore, it teaches the value of fostering relationships with any youngsters in the family by providing a solid example of dedication and prioritising.

Chapter Summary

The critical significance of arranging time for your spouse within the framework of a marriage emphasises how these efforts go beyond simple time management to address the psychological and emotional health of the union. It emphasises that prioritising the quality of connections above the number and emphasising the importance of cherishing the relationship is reflected in making time. The book offers smart methods for managing time well in a relationship, like proactive planning, cutting back on technology, setting aside time for one another, enjoying special occasions together, and remaining accommodating and considerate of one another's needs. It also discusses the many advantages of spending time together, such as improved communication, a firmer basis for trust, and forming happy memories.

Important Points

The Value of Time in Marriage: Realising that spending time with your spouse demonstrates your level of commitment and is vital to the longevity of your union.

Quality vs. Quantity: Stressing that meaningful and purposeful interactions make time spent together important since they help people connect on a deeper level.

Active Scheduling and Digital Detox: Promoting thoughtful scheduling of time spent together and the creation of technology-free areas to guarantee an uninterrupted, high-quality connection.

Shared Experiences: Emphasise the value of having shared interests and pastimes to improve communication and cooperation within the marriage.

Flexibility and Understanding: Emphasises the value of accommodating one another's schedules and the beneficial effects of individual development on a partnership.

Important Takeaways

Emotional and Psychological Well-being: Making time for your partner is primarily about prioritising the relationship's emotional health and displaying significant care and dedication.

The Temporal Structure of Marriage: Realising that there are various aspects to marriage time and that meaningful and purposeful time is when the strongest ties are created.

The Function of Technology: Understanding how digital gadgets impact relationships daily and how purposeful detachment is necessary to promote real connection.

The Importance of Shared Experiences: Hobbies and mutually enjoyable interests enhance lives and are essential components of a more solid marriage.

The Converging Benefits of Setting Time Apart: Spending time together builds the foundation of the relationship, improves communication, and sets a positive example for the kids in the household.

Practical Exercises

Weekly Planning Session: Set aside a certain amount of time each week to discuss and plan future activities you will be involved in, including those of both partners.

Establish regular "technology-free" evenings when all electronic gadgets are put away, and the emphasis is placed on in-person interactions or group activities.

Take Up a New Interest Together: Select a novel pastime or pursuit to investigate jointly, cultivating a spirit of exploration and cooperation within your partnership.

It's important to develop a daily habit of checking in with each other. Maintaining a strong connection and regularly checking each other's well-being is important. Take a few minutes to discuss your feelings, ideas, and experiences from the day.

Monthly reflection and adjustment meetings should be held to review the time spent together, talk about what went well and what may be improved, and modify plans as necessary to meet the requirements of both partners.

Reflection Time

About our daily schedules, how do we now prioritise our relationship, and what can we do better?

_____
_____
_____
_____
_____
_____
_____
_____
_____
_____
_____
_____
_____

How have digital gadgets impacted our quality of time together, and what steps can we take to lessen its effects?

Samantha Nunez Chapman

How can we strengthen our bond and maximise our time together by engaging in common interests or hobbies?

How do we properly express and compromise on our respective needs when it comes to alone time versus time spent together as a couple?

Samantha Nunez Chapman

While we reflect on our happy times, how might we improve them to cement our bond further?

CHAPTER TWENTY-FIVE

Start Sex

WHEN IT COMES TO MARRIAGE, THE BEGINNING OF INTIMACY is essential to a successful union. Beyond its apparent physical aspects, initiating sex has deep psychological and emotional undertones. This talk provides practical tips and real-life examples for initiating physical intimacy in relationships for newlyweds, seasoned partners, and individuals seeking to improve their relationships.

Not only is having sex an act in and of itself, but it also symbolises vulnerability and communication. "I desire you, I trust you, and I want to connect with you on a deeper level" is conveyed with this gesture. Although it takes courage and confidence for many, this step is essential to maintaining marriage's emotional and physical ties.

It's critical to comprehend the language of desire in your marriage. Individuals use this phrase in many different ways. Some people communicate their readiness and interest verbally, while others may receive their invitation through physical contact or particular gestures. The secret is to pay attention to your partner's cues and communicate in a way that suits them. It's about creating a secure environment where partners can freely communicate their needs and wants.

The idea of spontaneity and creativity is at the heart of practical counsel from the real world. It doesn't always take a big show to start a romantic relationship; often, the little, unplanned moments ignite passion. A last-minute kiss before heading out to work, a seductive letter tucked into a pocket, or a softly spoken praise could all be examples. These impromptu actions weave layers of suspense and thrill into the fabric of your personal life.

However, initiating sex also necessitates a profound comprehension of timing and context. It's critical to discern when your spouse is open to you and when they require space. This tenderness highlights how crucial emotional intelligence and empathy are in a marriage. It's a harmonious dance of respect and longing on both sides, not simply about your want.

Real-world examples show the variety of strategies for starting a sexual relationship. Please look at a marriage where one spouse uses vocal affirmations to express how much they feel wanted. In this instance, verbally conveying the need for intimacy and showing desire through praises can significantly accelerate the initiation process. On the other hand, for people who are more attuned to physical contact, the first steps in a sexual encounter could be a soft touch, a backward hug, or a massage that builds to a more personal embrace.

Furthermore, addressing issues like conflicting libidos or the effects of weariness and stress is critical. Here, communication is essential; being transparent about your needs and desires helps reduce miscommunication and promote more satisfying sexual relationships. To ensure that both partners feel valued and desired, strategies like planning intimate time or developing rituals that indicate readiness for intimacy can help close the desire gap.

Starting a sexual relationship is essentially an artistic endeavour that combines physical and emotional intimacy. Recognising and honouring one another's needs, preferences, and limits is essential. Couples can create a stronger, more satisfying bond by accepting vulnerability, being honest with one another, and carefully kindling the spark of desire through initiation. This chapter, which is devoted to the art of initiating sexual relations, is not just about improving physical closeness but also about fortifying your marriage.

Chapter Summary

The important part of starting a sexual relationship during a marriage is emphasising that it's not just a physical act but also a deep expression of emotional and psychological connection. It provides a sophisticated examination of the vocabulary of desire, the value of spontaneity, and the requirement of appreciating and complying with each partner's demands and limits. "To assist couples in improving their intimacy and strengthening their marriage." useful tips, real-world examples, and techniques for conquering typical obstacles like mismatched libidos are provided.

Important Points

Beyond its physical aspect, starting a sexual relationship is a potent way to communicate desire, trust, and a readiness to build a close bond with your partner.

Developing a satisfying sexual relationship requires understanding the language of desire, which is the ability to identify and react to each partner's distinct signs of intimacy, whether they be verbal, physical, or otherwise.

The Function of Creativity and Spontaneity: Little, impulsive actions can heighten a relationship's romantic and passionate elements and maintain the burning desire.

Timing and Context are Critical: For both parties to be satisfied, knowing when to start a sexual relationship and taking into account your partner's receptivity and general mood are essential.

Conquering Obstacles with Honest Communication: Whether it's divergent libidos or the effects of weariness and stress on one's sex life, honest communication about needs, wants, and challenges is essential to conquering them.

Important Takeaways

Vulnerability Is Strength: initiating sexual activity and displaying vulnerability deepens the emotional connection between partners, fostering closeness and trust.

Personalised Approaches to Intimacy: Recognising and honouring each partner's preference is essential when it comes to sexting; there is no one-size-fits-all approach to starting a relationship.

Regular and fulfilling sexual encounters are essential for a strong and happy marriage since they enhance the general well-being of both parties.

Emotional Intelligence Enhances Intimacy: Partners with high Emotional Intelligence are better able to negotiate the nuances of sexual intimacy and have more pleasurable interactions.

Being Intimately Creative Prevents Stagnation: Using spontaneity and creativity to start a relationship keeps it from stagnating and ensures a fulfilling and dynamic sexual life.

Practical Exercises

Desire a diary: For a week, each partner records in their "desire diary" the times they felt the need for closeness and the circumstances around those feelings. Share and discuss these notes to learn more about each other's cues.

Over a month, set yourself the challenge of being more spontaneous when it comes to initiating sex. "This can refer to performing unexpected actions, saying words that were not planned, or engaging in spontaneous behavior."

Intimacy Scheduling: To balance structure and unpredictability, schedule frequent "intimacy dates" but leave the details to the whims of the moment.

Exercise in Empathy: Spend a week observing your partner's nonverbal signs to gauge their attitude and level of intimacy without speaking to them.

Encourage open communication about desires and boundaries by holding a weekly talk about your sexual connection. Please focus on the positive aspects and suggest areas for improvement.

Reflective Time

Initiating sex with my partner: how do I feel about it, and what hidden emotions does it bring up for me?

_____
_____
_____
_____
_____
_____
_____
_____
_____
_____
_____
_____
_____

Given my partner's distinct language of love and desire, how can I better express my desire for intimacy with them?

_____
_____
_____

Samantha Nunez Chapman

How can we incorporate more creative components into our daily routine, and what function does spontaneity play in our private lives?

What differences in expectations do we have from one another, and how do our unique experiences and backgrounds affect how we approach making the first move towards sex?

Samantha Nunez Chapman

After considering our private interactions, how can we better match our actions to meet each other's needs and wants to strengthen our bond and sense of fulfilment?

Samantha Nunez Chapman

LEND YOUR VODY OUR VOICE

YOUR VOICE IS A DISTINCT THREAD WOVEN THROUGHOUT LIFE, rich with hues of wisdom and experience. As you close the book "How To Be A Better Wife And Improve Your Marriage," reflect on how your relationship has evolved as a result of your trip through its chapters. Did Samantha Nunez Chapman's advice cause a shift in your marriage, or did it open your eyes to new possibilities?

We are at a turning point in our lives where the power of sharing can help others find their way through their marriage journeys. Please think about writing an Amazon review if this book has had an impact on your life. Your thoughts can lead, uplift, and console those on similar journeys, whether they resound through the great halls of triumph or murmur in the peaceful nooks of introspection.

Maybe you know a friend, family member, or coworker who is about to embark on their own journey towards a more meaningful and happy relationship. Talking to them about your thoughts on this book can be the lighthouse that helps them find their way.

Your review, a patchwork of your ideas and encounters, not only honours the knowledge in these pages but also joins the chorus of voices singing individual songs of development, love, and challenge. Let's compose a symphony that reflects the harmonics of strengthened bonds and fuller lives.

So please, take the time to tell your tale. Your thoughts are priceless, whether they are shared in a quiet coffee chat or aloud from the peaks of the mountains. Post a review on Amazon and allow your insights to guide others through the sometimes stormy, always lovely sea of marriage.

Samantha Nunez Chapman

ACKNOWLEDGEMENT

THE PAGES YOU'VE READ HAVE BEEN WOVEN WITH A TAPESTRY OF voices and hearts contributing to this trip. This book, my labour of love, results from an eclectic symphony of spirits from the depths of introspection to the summits of inspiration.

To my family, Jake, my unwavering journey partner, whose warmth and wisdom light my way; Shalom, Samara, and Asher, our darling children, whose curiosity and laughter fill my days with wonder and delight. Their unwavering support and love are the foundation of who I am. You are the tune that complements my aspirations and keeps me rooted in our common past while inspiring me to aim higher. I've been reminded of the importance of connection by your tears and laughter, which have painted the background of this project.

To my group of friends, you have been my brilliant kaleidoscope of viewpoints and my sounding board for my wildest ideas. You have also given me constructive criticism that is delivered with kindness and encouragement that fills me in when I'm feeling doubtful. Our discussions, which cover everything from the serious to the everyday, have been the kindling that has ignited my imagination and pushed me to venture into unknown waters bravely.

The text was made accurate and comprehensive with sincere gratitude to the experts who contributed their knowledge. Thanks to your direction, I could confidently and curiously sail the enormous seas of knowledge, which was a beacon of light in the complex process of study and verification.

I am very appreciative of my mentor, whose knowledge is beyond words. Your advice is like a lighthouse—it shows me the way through the mist of uncertainty and enables me to stand out among the ordinary chorus.

Thank you for joining me on this adventure, dear reader. Your involvement brings these pages to life, turning static text into a dynamic conversation. This book is not a monologue but a dialogue spanning the breadth of our common humanity.

This acknowledgement is a modest way of saying thank you to everyone who helped, directly or indirectly, with the production of this book. Together, we've created a tapestry that is more resilient to your strands and richer in colour. We appreciate you being a part of this journey and helping us create a story that hopes to elevate, inspire, and resonate.

ABOUT THE AUTHOR

MEET SAMANTHA NUNEZ CHAPMAN, THE COMPASSIONATE RELATIONSHIP and marriage expert who has transformed countless homes and saved marriages from the brink of divorce. With a heart of love and a passion for building strong, thriving relationships, Samantha has become a beacon of hope for couples seeking lasting happiness.

Based in the vibrant city of Chicago, Samantha brings her own experiences and a deep understanding of human connection to her work. Her journey to becoming a relationship expert was born out of personal struggles and triumphs, giving her a unique perspective and unwavering empathy for those navigating the complexities of love.

With Samantha's guidance, couples find solace in her unwavering support and wealth of knowledge. She empowers them to explore the depths of their relationships, uncovering hidden strengths and addressing underlying issues that often go unnoticed. Samantha's approach is not about quick fixes or temporary solutions but about fostering deep-rooted transformation that paves the way for lifelong happiness.

Through her captivating writing and insightful teachings, Samantha inspires individuals to see beyond their immediate challenges and embrace the true potential of their partnerships. Her words resonate deeply, drawing readers into a world where love and understanding triumph over conflict and despair.

But Samantha's expertise extends far beyond the written page. She is an engaging speaker, captivating audiences with her infectious energy and relatable anecdotes. Whether speaking at conferences, hosting workshops, or counselling couples one-on-one, Samantha's ability to connect personally sets her apart as a trusted guide on the journey to harmonious relationships.

Outside of her professional pursuits, Samantha cherishes her loving family, who testify to the power of love and commitment. They drive her unwavering dedication to helping others create homes filled with joy, understanding, and unbreakable bonds.

So, if you're ready to embark on a transformative journey that will forever change the course of your relationships, allow Samantha Nunez Chapman to be your guiding light. Together, let's rewrite your love story and build a home that stands the test of time.

Samantha Nunez Chapman